A

THESE
UNITED
STATES

THESE UNITED STATES

PHOTOGRAPHS BY
FRED J. MAROON
TEXT BY
HUGH SIDEY

EPM
Publications
•
Hawthorn

This book is dedicated to my wife, Suzy, and our
children, Marc, Anne Hermine, Sophia, and Paul.
F. J. M.

To Edwin John Sidey, III, so that he will better
understand his land, his trust.
H. S.

FROM SEA TO SHINING SEA

We can span this country now with one gargantuan stride in a super-jet. From my home near Washington, D. C., to Hawaii is 10 hours and some 5,000 miles, about 35,000 pounds of fuel and a bottle of rich, red burgundy from the Napa Valley.

The time is obliterated and the miles reel off effortlessly into the fading mist of space that has just been. The fuel turns into an invisible trail of hydrocarbons and the burgundy is transformed into warmth and memory as one slides along that cold, thin arc. It was an afternoon not all that long ago when I took the journey, rising with immense thunder over the Potomac Valley, then heading into a sun that rimmed my far horizon but was still high in the Pacific sky. We would almost keep pace with the sun, we would exceed the measure of the old song "from sea to shining sea" by that much again. I do not mean to suggest at this time of writing that all I put down here occurred to me on that one flight. Time has enlarged my memory and led me to other thoughts, which is the privilege of a writer. I have tried to make that plain. But it was a remarkable interlude.

I confess to being a romantic. And flight still is an adventure. Every time I am in a plane and it lifts off the runway something of my old and constrained self is left back there on the ground. My spirit grows lighter as the plane climbs and events and people, time and space shrink into one view, like chapters of a history book spread out to read. The rivers tell of early explorations and settlement. The valleys and mountains sometimes shake out thoughts of battles of our wars. The cities are the watermarks of advancing civilization. The great men of history rise again—adventurers, merchants, statesmen, generals, writers. They come out on the stage below on foot and in canoes and on horseback and in their Model T's. I have been struck several times at how many of the articles in the giveaway magazines of the airlines deal with this kind of nostalgia and I suspect that whether they know it or not those writers and editors are responding to the same inner stirring.

On this flight there was something very special. It formed the framework for this essay on a nation, a people and a land that I really know so little about, but love so much. That is another part of this fantasy of mine when in the clouds—the lament about how many people I do not know, how many stories of great importance that I have never been told or read, how many places of beauty and fascination are only names or shapes on the horizon, passed by in a few seconds, replaced by others. It is a lament that fades with the distance, fortunately. There is so much.

I remember this journey with a clarity and a poignancy of none other that I have taken. From some strange chemistry my thoughts for most of that long twilight were on the land and its meaning, a meditation of literally hours. Height lessens the scars, dims the ugliness with almost anyone who wishes to be lifted out of himself. I have seen it bring color back into the faces of this nation's Presidents, my special study, as they soared over their troubles. Scowls have turned to smiles and once again as the surface receded the problems of America seemed manageable. Someday, perhaps, a scholar will write of the therapeutic effect of airplanes on men of power. It is not hard to imagine the deep religious stirrings that astronauts felt as they fled from the earth and it shrank into a blue and white orb in their windows.

There was suddenly a parade of the men about whom I had written in two decades. Presidents are a distillation of America. Dwight Eisenhower, out of Abilene, Kansas. I had been in his Gettysburg office a few weeks before his death and listened to a litany of wonder from him about what this nation had given him. John Kennedy, the Bostonian with the love for the sea. I had been in Dallas when he died and the world changed in an instant. I still could not fully comprehend that mad day. Lyndon Johnson, of Blanco County, Texas. There was a man to savor.

He was like the Rocky Mountains, born of some elemental force from within the earth. Fundamental, but flawed, a mixture of the frontier and the space age, a man of great angers and greater compassions, an energy so relentless that it would destroy itself finally while reaching for immortality. But he was rooted. That was good. He had grown up and smelled and tasted the soil of his parents, he had loved and hated, struggled and lost and won. Richard Nixon was curiously unrooted despite his claims of fondness for California. His goal was power; he was a product of the southern California scramble for wealth and position, a believer in the perpetual mirage of ambition peculiar to those golden climes. He went where he had to go—California, Washington, California, New York, Washington. He did what he thought he had to do. But he was never anchored geographically or intellectually, a drifting alien in a land he glorified with his Hollywood hyperbole. Gerald Ford was the profile of Grand Rapids, Michigan. Part Eagle Scout, part football player, part young Ivy League lawyer, part member and leader of Congress. "A Ford not a Lincoln," he said about himself and then set a style to show that he meant it. Genial, kindly, he was a rough political combatant but one who wiped the slate clean after every encounter. His was the way of compromise—give a little to get a little, go along to get along. It came from those modest streets of the middle land where people gear their lives to each other and the hardy outdoors they relish.

The plane banked back over Washington and it was aglow in the fading light. It sprawls as far as the eye can see and comes to a focus on the Mall with the Capitol, the Washington Monument and the Lincoln Memorial. Along that thin rectangle of land, in the White House, in the great, grey buildings of the government, almost all of the official life of this country has been conducted. The impression is not one of age, but youth. Strange, that I could feel such a kinship to those floodlighted monuments, to the crusted green statues that lurked beneath the arched branches of bare trees. The day before Kennedy became President, I flew with him back to Washington from Florida. He had been a friend before the great political crusade of 1960 and this was a last meeting before the Presidency consumed him. He was working on his inaugural address and he had

P 9   Where the sun first rises on America. Rocks and sea at Acadia National Park, Maine.

Pp 10-11   Morning on the Darby Dan Horse Farm near Lexington, Kentucky. Four stallions roam in their beautiful domain.

Pp 12-13   Ripening wheat beneath Montana's big sky. The vast panorama of plenty is on the Fort Peck Indian Reservation near Frazer.

Pp 14-15   The Cathedral Spires Mountain Range near Fairbanks, Alaska, march off, rank on snow-covered rank, in this October portrait.

P 16   The afternoon surf and sun blend in a thunderous natural symphony at Pfeiffer Beach, Big Sur, California.

scribbled some of it on a yellow legal pad. He tossed it to me and asked me to read the lines. I couldn't make out the handwriting and he quickly saw my difficulty, chuckled and took back the pad. Then he read. I cannot remember now exactly how they went, but I do remember he summed up his message: "What I want to say is that the spirit of the Revolution still is here, still is a part of this country." In less than half a year Kennedy would be in Vienna sitting across the table from the Soviet Union's Premier Nikita Khrushchev. "You're an old country, we're a young country," jibed Khrushchev in some strange twist of logic and history. "If you'll look across the table, you'll see that we're not so old," replied Kennedy.

From that time on I noticed the visible signs of our youth. Jackie Kennedy once talked about it. The last of the Civil War veterans had just died and that had made an impression on her. She wanted to start a project to preserve as much of our young history as possible. She turned the White House into a true museum and it goes on today, each family adding a small but distinctive touch.

Beyond the left wing of the plane, not too far distant, were the excavated foundations of Jamestown, the first settlement on this new land. It began in 1607. And not far from Jamestown was restored Colonial Williamsburg, source of so much of the thought that would shape our nation and its government in the following century. Only a few more miles away at Kitty Hawk was the monument to the first flight that took place in 1903, the ultimate distillation of those 300 years which followed after the three tiny ships had nudged up the James River to drop anchor and stay.

Never has there been such a dramatic human movement as the one that settled America. There was no barrier—not fear nor mountains, nor forests, nor emptiness, and finally not even the air. The world has never known such courage, such creativity and finally such abundance. Certainly it was the people who did it. But just as certainly it was this land that made it possible. No region on this earth has offered such a fruitful combination of resources and climate. There is nowhere such a rich variety of natural beauty flung across so great a distance. It is ours. It is young.

It is not without worry. As the folds of the Appalachians came into view, and the Shenandoah Valley with all of its melancholy history was below, questions about the future intruded. I had read the doomsday predictions of the Club of Rome, that we would run desperately short of food and raw materials within a hundred years. Others like Washington University's Barry Commoner had warned about how we would soon exhaust our clean air and fresh water unless we changed our ways. It is difficult to accept these extrapolations. There is something coldly analytical about them and they do not translate easily into the human experience. Yet, I have seen the scars we have left on our land. On almost any flight in the daytime one can see the buildup of smog over our metropolitan areas, the rivers turning dark and forbidding from the wastes poured into them. It is a warning. My feeling is that we teeter now on the brink. We can rescue ourselves and begin to heal our land, our nation. Or we can plunge on carelessly consuming ourselves into oblivion. We are beginning to anguish over the choice and that is the good sign. There still is more beauty than ugliness in this country, more untouched than destroyed. We must find a balance.

I have lost count of the times that I have traveled the eastern corridor from Washington to New York, the ultimate in megalopolis. By train, car and plane I have hurried back and forth. There are hideous stretches, dark and rotting buildings and so many acres of concrete that nobody has an accurate assessment of the area smothered. There are seven cities of more than a million population; a sixth of all Americans live there. But there are stretches where the eye cannot see any buildings or hear a truck. Near the arches of the Delaware Memorial Bridge nestles the small town of New Castle, Delaware, an 18th Century jewel that is beyond the stain of our mobile society. There are islands of purity that have not been claimed for housing developments; there are, even in the most congested areas, remarkable stretches of land that have been washed over by people but have been reclaimed with trees and grass. New Jersey is still 75 per cent agricultural by official designation. It is not hopeless. We need some national concept of land use, some better city planning (people planning, really) and most of all a better idea of the quality of life. We need new priorities. We need to sort out of the jumble of steel and glass what is good and that which helps free us for the pursuit of happiness we promised ourselves. We need, too, to take another look at the principles of human conduct on which we founded this nation and at the scale of human experience so eloquently expressed in the streets and backyards of Colonial Williamsburg, in the comfortable and manageable dimensions of New England's villages.

The movement is growing. There is a perceptible trickle back to the small towns, the evolution of shopping centers into true community centers, distant cousins of the old village green. There is some slight movement of people back into central cities and that may not be so much to lose identity but to find it in a neighborhood that is rebuilding, seeking to establish its own life and character within the bigger city, much as in London which is a city of villages.

The Bureau of the Census for almost 200 years has cranked out the statistics on our numbers and places of residence. Those incredibly wise and practical men who wrote our Constitution put it in there that we were to enumerate ourselves every 10 years, the first time in history a nation set in motion on the day of its founding a process of statistical profile. From those figures we have conceived of ourselves as a nation that almost instantly began the long, slow slide into an urban society, the balance tipping sometime in 1920. Now it is popular to point out that most of our people have clustered in three areas—along the eastern seaboard, around the Great Lakes and along the west coast, and to suggest that, like Europe, we will ultimately be a society of cities. In 1974, 75 per cent of the American people lived on 1.5 per cent of the land.

It was an easy assumption until Irving Kristol, an urban expert from New York University, took a look. He pointed out we may be headed toward an urban civilization without cities, a peculiarly American mutation. Only 30 per cent of the American people live in places with a population of more than 100,000, the layman's idea of what a city should be. This is just about the same as the number of people living in communities of less than 2,500 population, truly rural areas. The proportion of the people living in cities of more than a million is the same as it was in 1920. "The urbanization of America is thus more accurately described as the suburbanization of America," Kristol wrote in one of his treatises. The reason is that in the American heritage there is the strong assertion of space, a legacy of boundless land. Europeans built their cities to live in. Ours were utilitarian devices, conceived, sometimes furiously, says Kristol, for industry and commerce. The American preference has been and still is for non-city life, George Gallup confirms. One of his polls showed some 80 per cent of the American people preferred suburban, small town or rural life over city life.

As if to prove the point, in the middle of 1974 the demographers in the government came upon some new facts. They found that the movement of people back to small cities and towns of the United States had accelerated to the point that the rate of growth in the non-metropolitan areas had exceeded that in the large cities and suburbs. The change was recorded for the first three years in the 1970's and in demographic terms was one of the most dramatic shifts of direction in population of this century.

It does not mean that the people of the United States are going to be redistributed overnight. The large population centers are continuing to grow, but at reduced rates. What it could mean is that by the year 2000 we could reduce the degree of congestion in the metropolitan areas, bring a higher standard of living to many of the depressed rural areas. This change in population direction comes from the two obvious causes—disenchantment with city conditions and more jobs available in the smaller communities, which represents a dispersal of industrial concentration that has long been advocated by concerned sociologists.

So after coming together so frantically following World War II, we may have found that most of us never did want to be that close to each other, that we are still gripped by the earth. My suspicion is that a part of our inner urge is the desire to find a manageable size in our existence, to get a grip on our surroundings, to sink roots. Vance Packard, who diagnosed us in his book *A Nation of Strangers,* was not the first man to detect "a society of torn roots" that has produced a malaise of loneliness reflected in our songs and poetry, more seriously in shattered families and leaderless communities. "I have no doubt myself that one of the great unspoken forces in the life of Americans today is a longing for community, for human contact and human concern," wrote *The New York Times'* Anthony Lewis.

Wherever one turns there is new literature—and old—that beckons us to scale down our covetousness, to pause and come back to ourselves. There are limits to growth—emotional and intellectual as well as material. Donald Connery fled from New York and half a dozen of the world's great cities to settle in a small Connecticut town and he wrote a book about the rhythm and meaning of that life. His scripture was from Thornton Wilder's play, *Our Town,* which was about "the way we were: in our growing up and in our marrying and in our living and in our dying" in a tiny New Hampshire village at the turn of the century. Wilder said about his play that it was an attempt "to find a value above all price for the smallest events in our daily life." Connery found much of that value in his town and hinted that God surely had meant for people to live in such surroundings. "There are times," he wrote, "when I can bring myself to believe that a town like this one, far from being a relic of the past, is something of a model for the future . . . There is a visible yearning for a greater harmony of man and nature and for the intimacy of participation in a society of reasonable dimensions, whether a commune, a rural settlement, a New Town, an old town, or an aroused city neighborhood that has won for itself some measure of community control."

There are many Americans like Donald Connery. Annie Dillard moved to her solitary house in Virginia and wrote of the forces of nature with new beauty and depth. *Pilgrim at Tinker Creek* was a plea for the celebration of small deeds. Edwin Way Teale, the great naturalist, had wandered through these mountains and valleys gathering the material for his book, *North with the Spring.* He is one of the pied pipers of this time, his enticing song emerging from his study of nature's attention to detail. His following is immense. And I recalled his delight in reporting that a kindred spirit,

Thomas Jefferson, had kept meteorological records for decades, had classified Virginia's trees and animals, put down the comparative weights of squirrels and made a scientific report on fossils.

Jefferson and Washington fit their land. Or perhaps it is the other way around—they were formed by the fields and hills where they built their homes. Several times I have stood on the Monticello grounds and marveled at its graceful relationship to the surroundings. Jefferson could see the town of Charlottesville and the site of the University of Virginia, which held such a special place in his heart. He could see the high tree in front of the home of his friend James Monroe. Though far apart in distance by today's standards, there was a closeness among the early men of Virginia, who founded their lives on a harmony of ideas and purpose. I suppose it is the advantage of today's scholarship on Jefferson that left me with the notion that his buildings resembled the man. It is an idea that will not go away. They are not massive or gaudy, but lean and ingenious, devised to give pleasure and to use the phenomena of nature to enhance their comfort. It took Jefferson 40 years to complete Monticello as it stands today and of course it was not done even then. He certainly walks there now among the tourists, tinkering with his seven-day clock. He looks over his flowers and garden, surely, and sometimes stands and contemplates the giant poplar that he planted beside the house. Some modern historians scoff at the Jeffersonian doctrine that an agrarian society retains strength and independence and surely in this age it is an impossibility. But the idea still dwells in the American spirit.

The view from Mount Vernon, if anything, is more spectacular than that from Monticello. It has more sweep. The buildings have a little more bulk and independence. There is a dimension of loneliness that may suggest stubbornness. They are like George Washington, solid and enduring, an establishment that speaks of a way of life designed to be part of a great river, to shelter and protect and stand for all time. Washington must watch over his acres too, not as clever a man as Jefferson nor as curious, but stolidly marching through his holdings relishing good whiskey, good horses and with a vision as big as the view off his porch. Washington's character is implanted in ours.

I once read a small book about Washington crossing the Delaware and it lodged in my mind and re-emerged on my night flight, with the Delaware River not that distant on up the eastern seaboard. (It was a four-day horse ride for Washington but only a few minutes away by jet.) The river crossing and the battle of Trenton, both of which followed the dismal retreat from New York and New Jersey in 1776, prevented the total disintegration of the American Army and the American dream. It gave the new nation an immediate shot of hope and then through four long and bitter years of more defeat and confusion the memory helped sustain the thin cause. At the center was General Washington, his jaw set, his great frame enduring cold and disappointment and going on, always going on. On that Christmas Day he and his troops did cross the river amid slabs of ice, as the story goes. But they did not stand erect in the bow of the boat, flag flying as Emanuel Leutze painted the scene for generations of school children. Washington, like his men, was soaked through from sleet and rain. Once across the river he allowed no fires, sat down on an old beehive in a muddy pasture. That was headquarters. Everything went wrong. The crossing was hours behind. Support from other troops never materialized. The powder of the men was so wet they could not fire their muskets. When his officers came to him several times during the long night to ask if he wanted to change his plans, the General made a grimace that said no. In the dawn of the day after Christmas as the ragged troops marched half asleep and numbed from the cold, some still doubted Washington meant to attack. When General John Sullivan dared send an aide to ask again for orders, Washington cleared the air. "Tell him to advance and charge." The rout of the Hessians at Trenton is fixed in history, a mixture of providence and the granite resolve of the Virginian. It came in part from the valley of the Potomac.

On farther north was another river valley of special meaning to me—the Hudson River Valley. For a year following World War II, I was stationed in the army at West Point. Then, as a young reporter I had lived in Tarrytown, near Washington Irving's Sleepy Hollow. There is no river valley anywhere else in the world with the same sense of enduring majesty as the Hudson River Valley. I walked its rocky flanks in the winter months and felt the full chill of wind off slate-grey water. I picked blueberries in the summer and idled away hours simply looking at the colors that rippled through the mountains in the fall. History deepened the experience. West Point, a military stronghold long before an Academy, presided over the valley with a lofty authority and it was easy to see why the British wanted Benedict Arnold to sell the place out. I traced his wild flight from the point that British Major Andre was picked up by a couple of original GI's and they discovered the incriminating papers in his boot. It was a journey through the shadowy glens and over the river that had almost more fascination than some of the more noble enterprises in our history. I sensed in those months how at least a part of Franklin Roosevelt must have been formed. Surely some of his courage was rooted in those massive hills that came down to the water with such grandeur. Certainly, the sense of hope that he exuded came out of a reservoir that was generously filled by growing up at Hyde Park with the Hudson Valley and its cast of characters as his classroom.

It was no accident that Roosevelt was the man who reached out to the drought-stricken farmers of the midwest, one who placed preservation of the land high on his list of concerns. Minnesota's Hubert Humphrey was one of those so touched. Years after I left the Hudson, the Senator would movingly describe the moment. In the depths of the depression when the drought was most severe around his hometown of Doland, South Dakota, Humphrey's father loaded the young man into the family Model A. They went outside of town for a special event. Men from Washington had come to begin to plant the shelter belts, a New Deal concoction to help stem the dust storms. The scraggly pine seedlings were put into holes in the parched earth as the citizens of Doland stood in awe. Ultimately, the shelter belts were to form a strip 200 miles wide that would reach to the Texas panhandle. "I think all the trees were dead within a couple of weeks," the Senator recounted. "But it did not matter. For the first time the people out there felt that somebody cared about them." Hope has never languished long in this land.

Thomas Wolfe of North Carolina could write about it like nobody else.

As my plane climbed the last slopes of the Blue Ridge his shadow passed beneath the wings and I struggled to remember his words about October, which now as I write I can supply in their fullness. "Now October has come again which in our land is different from October in other lands," he wrote. "The ripe, the golden month has come again, and in Virginia the chinkapins are falling. Frost sharps the middle music of the seasons, and all things living on the earth turn home again. The country is so big you cannot say the country has the same October. In Maine, the frost comes sharp as driven nails, just for a week or so the woods, all of the bright bitter leaves, flare up: the maples turn a blazing bitter red, and other leaves turn yellow like a living light, falling about you as you walk the woods, falling about you like small pieces of the sun so that you cannot say where sunlight shakes and flutters on the ground, and where the leaves."

My plane fled on in that swift mission. The Appalachians fell behind us. The colors shifted in the far sky and then there were the incandescent tracings of the civilization below. Another world. There are the soft, glowing domes where the cities lie, the thin strands of highways that tie everything together—a gleaming illustration of our affluence. To hear Ben Wattenberg tell it in his book on *The Real America,* our national income is proof positive that the future is now. The evidence of the success of our way of life lies spread out before us, not perfect by any means, but a triumph rather than a tragedy, a great hope rather than a burden of guilt. Reading the census figures Wattenberg found, "Something special has happened in the United States in recent years that has never happened before anywhere; the massive majority of the population of a nation is now in the middle class." Almost 60 per cent of the people have a family income of more than $10,000 per year. That is a testament to problem solving, an indicator that our government, no matter its anguish of the last years, has worked. But solutions to problems bring other problems, a rule as old as human misery. Our problems are the problems of affluence and they will require new answers. "America," insists Wattenberg, "still has a winning hand and only a lack of confidence—confidence we realistically deserve to have in ourselves—can turn this nation into a loser."

There were other lights in the night that I had not noticed before. In between the villages and cities was a grid of the bright, blue mercury-vapor lamps, the signposts of farms. The family farms diminishing? Looking literally a hundred miles or more in all directions on this clear night I could see no end to the bright sentinels. They seemed everywhere, no remote patch of ground untouched, no dark crevice unowned. This was another seeming contradiction—a diminished farm population that yet seemed to engulf the land. Such are the fantasies from 37,000 feet.

When I crossed the Mississippi River there was the first feeling of coming home. I remain, despite two decades in Washington, a man of place—Iowa. Off in the southwest part of the state is the tiny farm town of Greenfield, its population 1,800 when I left. But it was still a state-width away and I renewed my casual vigil at the jet window. Mark Twain's river was a thick, dark streak down below, visible for the lack of those winking lights that clustered on its shores. What an incredibly lucky man Samuel Clemens was to have grown up on his bluff with those long summer days of the midlands in which to fish and roam, to free his imagination and to record those images in his wry style. I know from my family's experience that today's children have been inspired by the adventures in space. But for them the excitement rises and falls as each new probe comes along, a one-dimensional scene on the television tube. Perhaps because there was nothing else, Clemens and his generation turned their curiosity loose on what was around them. The mysteries of a river are infinite, the allure of islands no matter how small are irresistible. This inoculation flows in many veins today.

Within a few minutes after the Mississippi had been swallowed by the dark, the pilot of our plane announced that Des Moines was below and then I began to wonder if by some stroke of extraordinary luck I could see the outline of my home town. We were headed right and I began to pick out the land marks of those 60 miles between town and city. I had traveled it first in one of Henry Ford's Model A's, an endless journey into an alien environment, fascinated with its huge stores and office buildings and terrorized by its strange rituals of car parking and traffic lights. We were flying right down the groove of Highway 92 and the lights were the dots to which I drew imaginary lines. The familiar curves of the road were clearly discernible, bringing memories of how it felt to hurry by these landmarks coming home from college or on furlough from the Army, drawn in some inexplicable way to a tiny patch of ground with no special features or no special distinction. Home. Iowa. The United States. They flowed into one great mosaic of a million fragments.

Finally there was my town. I suspect now as I write that it was clearer in my mind than my eye, but that hardly matters. In the minute or so that it was in view I relived years in a singular flashback of events, people, sights, sounds and smells. In my years of subsequent wandering, I found that within most people there is a private drawer full of such stuff, whether they come from Texas or Connecticut, or New York City or Los Angeles; whether they are from the mountains or the plains or lived by the sea. John Kennedy would often point out that the percentage of salt in a man's blood was the same as in the sea, a sure sign that man was meant to be close to the oceans. I cannot claim that there is any similar chemistry for the prairies but I do claim that whatever it is, the sense of this nation that rises from these places is of a remarkably consistent texture. Of course, some areas and some people were blighted, distorted and rejected. But the special strength of this nation comes from those things which touched most—a sense of freedom, of common dignity and a land that would provide.

My eyes in a few swift seconds swept up and down the streets of Greenfield seven miles below. There was my uncle's filling station on the edge of town, still pumping gas. Yes, it was only about 8 p.m. and there would be business. The gas station is a peculiarly American institution, a cultural stop for small boys with bicycles and ones a little older with cars. I wondered how many American males had got their first taste of tinkering at the corner station, been counseled in the art of tire changing, brake tightening and of course the mechanics of sex. Instantly the greasy faces of the boys at the station that I had known leaped to mind and I wondered if any of them were still there scrubbing windshields and offering advice on squeaks and rattles, then ducking into the warmth of the station to smoke and joke. Some were especially lustrous, like the high school football stars. Almost all of them, as I recall, went off to World War II and a few of them never returned. I vaguely remember the notices that ran in my father's newspaper of battlefield deaths, of graves that still bind us to France and New Guinea and a hundred other places. That, too, is an American litany.

The white steeple of the Presbyterian church poked above the huddle of modest houses. It struck me again, as it had so many times before, how much I owed that small church for the sense of some greater authority that I had carried all these years and far more. The idea that history could add meaning to our lives first came clear in the Bible stories from an endless procession of Sundays in the cramped rooms of the Sunday School that were too hot or too cold. Somehow it found its way into the dim recesses of a blockaded and protesting mind but it did not assert itself for years. I heard the first of Bach and Beethoven on the old church organ and was an instant if inexpert captive. There was beauty and genius in sound and it was for anybody who cared to listen, even something to duplicate no matter how crudely on our mail-order trumpets and flutes. It is a curious conviction of mine today that the Bible led me into science and mathematics which I pursued with some zealousness for a few years. I can recall trying to bring some kind of visualization to the idea of everlasting life which was the reward so graphically contrasted with eternal damnation. I would lie in my bed at night and there would form in my mind concentric rings of consciousness that rippled on and on. I would race ahead of them, hoping to reach a point so distant that I could look back and see it all. But I could never capture anything but darkness before I subsided into sleep. For a time I thought that there would be some diagram or some chart or at least a theory in my battered school texts that would tidy up this awesome concept but I never found it. And there were too many new adventures to pursue with each morning's light to worry very long.

The old town square with its red brick courthouse was easily discernible, the stores where I had poked and wandered before and after school. If there was a season more exciting than the start of school I did not realize it until I became 12 years old. School meant new pencils, new tablets, certainly a new book or two and if one was lucky a new pair of tennis shoes. My Presbyterian conscience hovered near the surface ready to squelch an excess of joy over such possessions. But I must confess that American acquisitiveness triumphed. I felt unabashed pleasure at buying something new. The two times the family got a new car, there was unbounded ecstasy. I have assumed as my knowledge of this world and the men who made it mounted that this subterranean urge was not far from the same thing that possessed John D. Rockefeller or Andrew Carnegie and had I been in Cleveland when the Rockefeller oil holdings were burgeoning or Pittsburgh when steel was becoming the national nourishment that I would have responded in the same fashion to the limit of my ability and elastic Presbyterianism. The guilt rode on my shoulder (rather lightly) over two decades until I read a piece by one of the great advertising tycoons of our time. It was an exhortation to recapture the joy of buying and owning. Apparently this man had been frightened by the wave of anti-materialism which had swept college campuses and his memories, like mine, were not of evil but sweet satisfaction. Yet, this is the seed, unrestrained and fed to bursting, of much of our trouble today.

I marveled at my window again about the country's youth. Most of the stores on the Greenfield square I knew by heart. Most of them were still owned and operated by the people whom I had known as a boy, many of them not much changed over 30 years. Much had happened in and around my life in that time, and yet I was confronted with the fact that just as much of me was the same. I have watched five Presidents in Washington and it was the same with them. No matter how complex the issues before them, no matter what the advice they got from others, their actions almost always arose from the inner impulses which were formed by the small beginnings of their lives. Dwight Eisenhower's sense of decency and honor, his strongest trait, came from his family in Abilene. John Kennedy was nourished in the history of Boston and it flavored his outlook. Lyndon Johnson never forgot the legend of the Alamo which was told to him before he went to school. It was, I suspect, the same with Richard Nixon, a mixture of triumph and tragedy. And Gerald Ford is an open and obvious product of Grand Rapids. There is a history of money and luxury by now in America, but there is no aristocratic legacy. The history of the grandfathers and the great grandfathers who founded the fortunes are too fresh, their human dimensions too well known, their rascalities too strongly suspected (or proved) to provoke much worship. This is, as Thomas Jefferson wanted it to be, a society largely based on achievement.

My eyes found a dark wedge down a side street off the town square—the newspaper shop of my family. I could hear the presses heave and groan on Wednesday night when the final pages were printed. I could feel again the flat sheets of newsprint slip through my fingers as I fed them into the old folder that sometimes simply refused to work and delayed the town's Wednesday evening routine. My father, with his persistently cheerful face, showed up, a mechanical genius who could by sheer cunning coax any recalcitrant creature back into production. These were such small things in the print shop, but so heavily freighted with the lasting sense of obligation. Up until a few years ago, we did not worry much about the significance of work. Whatever one did was necessary and needed as America grew—a gross national product measured first in millions, then billions, and now a trillion. Most of the industrialists and business executives whom I have met in the country have felt at some time in their formative years the sense of achievement which I felt in that little newspaper plant. They run America now. But those coming behind them have not always had the sense of fulfillment that they have had. It is another of those fading meanings that must be revived, another reason to rescale ourselves to reality.

There was always an undertow of obligation in my town, part of the cement of society that is in such a short supply now. It was relentless, affecting the uninspired and the unaspiring as well as the self-starters. I have often wondered how many children from these tiny communities were pushed into productive lives, whereas they might have languished in urban indifference. There was no excuse for not playing football if you weighed 150 pounds or more and were reasonably sure of foot. You were expected to answer the call to scrimmage. If the church choir needed a tenor or a baritone, no matter how much your voice was in the throes of puberty, that too was a duty which was not lightly ducked. Or if the marching band needed a trombone the recruiting program was oblivious of social status, wealth and sometimes native ability. Trombone players were somehow found. It was not unusual in this rural renaissance to see the star quarterback duck out of the half time pep talk and put on his band uniform, march down the field for a turn or two playing the trumpet, then hurry back into his shoulder pads.

One's presence at town celebrations was expected. Lending a hand for cleanup campaigns, tree planting programs, scrap metal and used paper drives was another part of the civic duty that seemed to be instilled at birth. And in times of tragedy, there was a rigid rule that was never written and rarely spoken but it operated on any person over the age of 10— you went to help those in trouble. I remember in all its horrifying detail the afternoon that three of my friends and myself were called from a freshman high school class to go render artificial respiration to a man who had collapsed in a desperate effort to save his burning machine shop. We labored over the lifeless body for an hour knowing it was hopeless but driven by the understanding that we were the only ones who had taken a Red Cross course in life saving and thus must do something to be worthy of that trust until a doctor could be found. And even when the verdict of death was given we went on trying to revive one of our own.

We have even made death a special problem now. It is isolated, hidden, barely acknowledged in our modern mysticism. Many are not prepared for it. In tiny communities like mine, death was a part of life, introduced into the rituals of growing up along with the ten commandments and the preparations for a career. There was sorrow, to be sure, but less fear, an acceptance of this natural cycle ordained by some higher power.

Out of it all, I am now convinced, came not only a sense of one's abilities and duties but a realization that others could be depended upon. The simple formula of giving trust to get trust is another of those fading virtues, illustrated to a shattering degree by the tragedy of Watergate where Richard Nixon and his men founded their power on suspicion and hate and in the end lost the trust they coveted. The singular success of small-town men and women in business stems from this understanding that manifests itself in delegating authority, sharing confidence and nurturing the ability of all those around them.

The plane began to slant away from the old town and I darted here and there with my eyes. The high school was built when my grandfather was head of the school board. It was still a proud building, the biggest in town. A half block away hidden in the crowns of huge elms and maples, so dense that even without leaves I could not see through them, was my small home. It was winter and there were grandchildren near and that had always been my mother's first duty—to warm others, to minister to almost any reasonable whim and some not so reasonable. I have not found grandmothers diminished by Woman's Lib or automatic washers. The urges survive. In Laguna they play the piano for old songs and in Chevy Chase they go ice skating and in Greenwich they have been known to crew in the sloop races.

My children have heard their grandmother tell how she rode a pony to teach in a one-room school near the Winnebago Indian Reservation in Nebraska. When a blizzard froze the barn door where her horse was kept during her teaching hours, she was seized with terror at being caught in the storm. Two Indians loomed out of the snow, battered the door open. She never forgot it and the few dollars she could save from the household money went off regularly to those desperate Indian schools that send the poorly printed appeals. It was no burden. It was a thank-you.

One day when I was home she handed me a small book called *Buggies, Blizzards and Babies*. It was written by Cora Frear Hawkins, a woman in her eighties, about her father who had been a doctor in Sloan, Iowa, before the century turned. "He delivered me," my mother said. I read the thin volume and there was another of those reminders of our brief history. Dr. Edwin Frear had crossed the ice-filled Missouri in a boat, had barely escaped a raging prairie fire, and had driven his buggy on country calls across land unmarred by fences.

The spring in Iowa was everything—but nothing so much as the deep pungency of turned earth. Tucked away in my brain is a vignette of hurrying from school in the gathering dusk to be beside my father as he spaded our small vegetable garden. I was stirred and drawn by the aroma of renewal. The fall was an olfactory treat too. The first tang of burning leaves signaled a beginning of its kind. For a small boy it heralded a series of new delights that would unfold through the weeks climaxing in Christmas. With the bonfires came ripe apples—MacIntosh and Jonathan—that matched the tartness of the weather. There were wiener and marshmallow roasts to celebrate the approach of Halloween. And on that night there were mysterious events which brought delicious merriment. In the dead of night—no one seemed to know how or by whom—great arrays of farm machinery showed up on the town square and in the school yards. Manure spreaders, harrows, rakes, wagons and tractors made their way to the places of honor. Year after year until the world grew too serious for such things, those tolerant farmers came to town the next day to claim their machinery and denounce the rascals who did it. The time a goat was suspended from the flag pole and the year a horse showed up in a teacher's office were moments of special relish that brought a week's wonder and laughter. Years later while visiting the Allegheny College Campus in Pennsylvania I heard a story about one of the school's students who in 1860 had distinguished himself by helping to hoist a calf into the college tower. His name was William McKinley, and he became the 25th President of the United States.

Not all my prairie memories were pleasant. The hot winds of the drought years numbed my senses. They blew remorselessly out of the south, turning the pastures a brittle brown, curling the leaves on the elms and oaks, finally sucking the farm ponds dry. The earth itself under the scorching sun turned into rock and split between the rows of shriveled corn. We would look anxiously in those years of the mid-1930's for clouds. They rarely came and when they did they were fragile and barren, giving way themselves to the heat and dust. Not even the night brought the cool. Electric fans hummed from the tables and chests. Our mattresses were hauled down from the stifling upstairs rooms and put on the living room floor and the sheets were sprinkled lightly with water.

Then the grasshoppers came, clouds of them, swarming from every field, eating almost everything in sight including the paint off the houses. The winters were furious too. The snow came early, at first a great joy, but then it piled up and refused to melt. The temperature plunged to 20 degrees below zero and stayed there. Pipes froze, so did livestock caught in the blizzards. The sledding was superb but as the cold held on interest died. The frigid air knifed through one's lungs on the laborious treks up the long hills and toes and fingers numbed quickly.

Yet, in the mind of a child well loved and never hungry, such hardships were almost more of an adventure than a burden. I was far away from the worlds of those unshaven drifters who came off the rail lines and sat on the back steps begging for a free meal. Not until later did I comprehend the tragedy in the eyes of those men and women who came to my father, the county's director of relief, for food and clothing.

And there was the thread of a sense of humor that somehow survived heat and cold, Herbert Hoover, the depression President, and even the grasshoppers. I remember the roars of laughter at a church supper when one farmer got up and said he had invented a foolproof plan for exterminating grasshoppers. "You take one block of wood," he said. "Get a grasshopper and put it on the block. Then, take another block of wood and slam it down on the first block. Keep doing that until you run out of grasshoppers."

Many of the men and women who lived in those years never fully recovered. Some of them drifted west. Others just waited in defeat for death. The human current went on, shifting slowly but perceptibly. But the land did not change that much. Some of it ran off with the rain into the rivers and some of it was used to store water as a hedge against drought. In the spring of most years there rose again the smell of rich earth. And in the autumn the trees continued their ritual of color, and bonfires filled the bared branches, filtering the sun into golden shafts.

There is, I suspect, somewhere in the human system a registry for all these sensations. They help mold a person when they are there and their absence leaves a mark. Frank Lloyd Wright, the great architect who hailed from Wisconsin, understood that in some way man was meant to be fused to a part of the natural environment. Wright let light and air into his structures and railed with his marvelous acidity against buildings, cities and societies that did not. The wisdom of his words now is more apparent as we struggle to preserve the links with nature.

Gone with my town were the alleys with all their mystery, the old barns with troves of junk, the swimming pool that came from WPA, the athletic field where I once caught a pass for an unneeded touchdown and dropped several for needed scores. I thought about how free a mind could be in America. There was no reasonable curiosity that could not be indulged, no ambition that could not be entertained for at least a moment or two. For a dollar we went up with the barnstormers for a ride in an open cockpit. One fall, our fifth grade teacher gave us hourly radio reports on the progress of the America's Cup races in Newport. Why were kids in the midst of the corn fields caring about the rich and their sport? Because the races were peculiarly American and so were we. The class broke into a hearty cheer when the word came that the Ranger had beaten Great Britain's Endeavour II. We kept the cup. And the fifth grade of the Greenfield Public Schools had done its bit. My interest in that competition was firmly fixed. From then on I followed every race.

All of this may be more of the meaning of this country than we know. America is a collection of small things done well. Our secret was to have no secrets, to work openly in concert, to perceive success and failure and do better. New York City is made of Chicago's idea for a skyscraper, Pittsburgh's steel girders, Vermont's marble and brains from Ohio, Pennsylvania, Missouri and every other state. Our danger lies in abandoning the formula.

From the Missouri River to the Rockies is the middle land of great distances. To me it has always been a land of history more than places. The people moved across it, fought over it, conquered its spaces with their strength and ingenuity but found few places to cluster and build large cities. The images in my mind were from reading about the region—thin lines of Indian warriors riding as if they were grown to their horses; long caravans of wagons lumbering west in the shimmering heat;

buffalo by the hundreds of thousands grazing along rivers, running ponderously in fright from hunters and storms; vast grass fires racing with the edge of the wind, consuming everything before them in a ritual of cleansing which was as useful as it was hideous.

The Mormons had come this way. Their long trail has been carefully marked by the descendants of those who had made that hard journey which began in the winter of 1846. It is one of the episodes in our history that speaks for so much else in the country it has become a valid symbol of all America. The Mormons began their march when they were denied the right to worship as they wished, a grotesque violation of one of the fundamentals of the Constitution. They left their homes in Nauvoo, Illinois, trudged across Iowa with their hand carts, gathering each night in their camp to sing of God and their own indomitable spirit. Perhaps they were singularly blessed to have suffered so much in their time. They made their journey, took a bleak land and turned it into wealth. Their pride and continuing success now rides on that legend of courage. In 1955 members of the sect came back to Omaha to help dedicate the Mormon Memorial Bridge built across the Missouri River at the spot where those first settlers wintered on their way west. I talked with one of the women who had come on this new pilgrimage. Her ancestors had been part of the first group to cross Iowa. One of them became ill and it was apparent he would not live. The caravan could not wait for those who were sick. So this woman's grandfather, then a 10-year-old boy, stayed behind to bury the man and came on with others to rejoin his family. The melancholy heroics of those people lives on in the music of the Mormon Tabernacle Choir. Only a few weeks before Kennedy was killed he visited the Tabernacle in Salt Lake City. Several times before he was assassinated he recalled how deeply the music had touched him.

On a brooding hill in Council Bluffs, Iowa, stands the preserved home of Grenville M. Dodge, a name that was hardly a household word. But he is the engineer who surveyed the route and supervised the building of the Union Pacific Railroad. From the front porch you can see far to the west where Dodge and his construction contractor, General John Casement, pushed the tracks that were the permanent inscription of Manifest Destiny.

From Sacramento, California, came the Central Pacific, its Chinese construction crews driven by James Strobridge and Charles Crocker, a 265-pounder described as "crude, loud, tactless and profane." The chorus of steel rang through the mountains and over the plains in what may have been the greatest epic of sheer muscle that the nation has produced, bringing the rails together in Utah, a final orchestration of raw strength and skill that put down as much as 10 miles of track a day. The story of the railroaders never got its full due.

Take the case of William Thompson, a young man working on the Union Pacific line in 1867. The telegraph wire along the track went dead in the night and he took a crew down the rails on a hand car and ran straight into an Indian ambush. He was clubbed, then scalped but the scalp with Thompson's long blond hair fell from the Indian's belt. Thompson saw it drop and crawled to get it, jammed it in his pocket. Then he stumbled on into the night toward the outpost of Plumb Creek. When he arrived there he still had his scalp. He was put on a special train, his scalp placed in a bucket of water and both were sent to Omaha 250 miles away to see if they could be put back together. It was too late for that; the scalp had been damaged too much to be restored. But Thompson recovered and went back to railroading minus his splendid hair.

There were others in this rite of space who were passed by too quickly when history was so swiftly written. One was Samuel Colt of Connecticut. On a day in 1838 or 1839 (nobody seems quite certain) a small band of Texas Rangers equipped with Colt's new revolvers met some Indians along the Pedernales. The Indians attacked, confident the whites would have to dismount to use their clumsy long rifles. The Indians' world fell in. The rangers jumped on their horses and ran the Indians down firing their Colts as they went. The battle for the West was decided.

The prairie was gone. Above the snow-packed Rocky Mountains my mind turned to other journeys in other years. I was always drawn west. It was as if the early hunters and the wagon trains that followed them had set up a magnetic field that continued to tug at those who came to live along the way. Between my junior and senior years in college a friend and I boarded an old Ford and headed toward Idaho. We arrived at Yellowstone National Park before the tourists and drank in this spectacle of geysers, falls, bears, the placid lake and the cold, clear air that crusted the water each morning with ice. It was my first heady taste of what I had read about and seen in single dimension. We drove through the Bitterroot Mountains and up into the Idaho panhandle, taking jobs with the Forest Service in the St. Joe Forest Reserve. It was yet another world. The space was no more impressive than what I had known, but from the mountains I could see nothing but the heavy forests of white pine. The blue-green undulations were unbroken—no towns or cities, only rarely a cabin on the edge of a mountain meadow where cattle were driven in the summer months.

I saw the sun rise over the Columbia River gorge between Oregon and Washington; then the great, sheer flank of El Capitan in Yosemite National Park. We walked in the redwood forests, our steps and our voices muted in wonder. One evening we stood on the lip of the Grand Canyon and watched the dark shadows fill up the chasm. Having seen such wonders I came back to my prairie home with a new restlessness, a wider and more profound view of how the nation was formed.

My plane was over the coast. The clusters of lights in California marked the end of land and beyond was the ocean. The people seemed to have piled up on that fringe, to have run out of space, each succeeding wave to have climbed on the shoulders of those before them until there were too many people and not enough air—finally the dreams ran thin. I pondered again one of my private wonderments about California's two great cities. San Francisco with all of its beauty and sophistication seemed so self-satisfied as to be on the edge of stuffiness, vaguely dull in its single-minded pursuit of the good life. Total pleasure seemed at times to be a civic responsibility. Something vital was missing. Los Angeles which had violated almost every premise of grace and sensibility was strangely exciting and alive, a city engaged in a struggle with the world and with itself. It was grotesque in many ways, but there was something unusually exhilarating about it.

The long miles of ocean were beneath us—hours of sheeted blackness, only a ship's light now and then to relieve the void. We were racing toward our farthest land, our newest frontier. Hawaii is unlike anything else in our experience. Heavily Asian in culture and climate, but Western in its ambitions, Hawaii added a new dimension of expectation to the American vision. The land looked toward the South Seas, Japan, Taiwan and mainland China. I wondered in that night if the future lay in China. I had been in Peking on the Monday night when Richard Nixon arrived. He stood in the front of the Great Hall at the Gate of Heavenly Peace with China's Chou En-lai and these two traditional enemies raised their glasses to each other and to peace while the People's Liberation Army Band Number One played *Turkey in the Straw*. We had renewed friendship of a sort with 800 million people, one fifth of the human race whom we had treated as non-existent for more than 20 years, one of those acts of political madness perceived only in hindsight. The new view of the world surely included those vast reaches of ocean and land. And yet I had come home from China wondering what it meant. I had dined the last night in Peking with a 40-year-old magazine editor. We had talked about our ambitions, our hopes. Although we could agree that we wanted peace and well-being for all mankind, we could not find any other common ground. Wealth was meaningless to him. Possessions were nuisances. Travel was not an ambition. He sought his satisfaction within himself. His sense of limited purpose and serenity was at once irritating to me and also appealing. Something in our current crisis of materials seems to be drawing us Americans in that direction.

Late in my long night we landed in Honolulu, its shore ablaze in the languid air. It had been a journey nearly a fourth of the way around the globe and still we were on American soil. Even now the memory is fresh and meaningful—a 10-hour epic of distance and feeling. I felt another layer of experience had been laid over the bedrock of my prairie days. In each of us character and outlook are built like a geologic formation out of the strata of time and events. After each new experience we begin another. There is no end, nor any escape, but always challenge. Now the challenge for all Americans is not to win a land or to enlarge it, but to preserve it.

MID-ATLANTIC STATES

DISTRICT OF COLUMBIA,
MARYLAND, PENNSYLVANIA, DELAWARE,
NEW JERSEY, NEW YORK

This is the mind—New York to Washington. Writers and Arizona politicians keep trying to deny it. Its confusion, crime and confrontation sometimes obscure its vital function. But the fact endures at the end of two centuries that the power lies in the mid-Atlantic states. There is money and government. The headquarters of mass communication is here. And the headwaters of imagination. Indeed, the intellectual collision of millions of talented people may be the area's greatest strength. The standards of American excellence in art, theater, literature, music are set and tested in a huge human caldron.

It attracts and it repels. It has grown so big and so complex that it snuffs out some of the human grace it glorifies. S. J. Perelman, the author and wit, went off from New York in 1970 pronouncing it no fit place for civilized people. He settled in London. In two years he was back in New York proclaiming "there is such a thing as too much couth." There is no accurate count of the number of defeated senators and congressmen who have clung to Washington just to savor the power they once shared.

There are too many people and too many buildings and too many highways crowded into the space but it is the nerve center of the nation, sending its signals out to everyone. They get up in the frozen Illinois mornings to learn what the Department of Agriculture has to say about corn and hogs. The brokers on the Pacific Coast gear their days three hours ahead to fit the stock market opening and closing in the crowded confines of Wall Street. Actors and musicians in Seattle and Chicago study the reviews from Broadway and the Lincoln Center. There is no rule that says it has to be that way nor even any claim that it is the best way to do things.

P 41   Giant bust of Abraham Lincoln by Gutzon Borglum presides over the U.S. Capitol Rotunda beneath the dome.

Pp 42-43   "Here, sir, the people govern"—Alexander Hamilton. The nation's Capitol in Washington.

P 44   The White House on a summer afternoon. It is museum, office and home, each President feeling its heritage, leaving his mark.

P 45   The Supreme Court building in Washington. It is the watchtower of American self-government.

Pp 46-47   Before there was a Washington, there was Georgetown. It is now a unique and vital section of the Capital.

P 48   The Washington Monument, laboriously built, carefully preserved.

But it is the way it worked out. We take our measure in mid-Atlantic.

The spirit of this Republic is assayed and renewed on the gentle slope of Washington where the Capitol, perhaps the nation's most beloved building, thrusts its massive iron dome above the city that spreads at its feet. Beneath that dome the aspirations of all 50 states are melded in the continuing ritual of democracy. Fred Maroon's camera, resting on the base of sculptor Gutzon Borglum's bust of Abraham Lincoln and pointed toward Constantino Brumidi's fresco, "The Apotheosis of Washington," captures the feeling in the Capitol Rotunda that still awes the legions of tourists who come each day. Lincoln lay in state there. So did John Kennedy, both part of the democratic procession watched over by Brumidi's mixture of gods and mortals. Brumidi troweled them in pigmented plaster in 1865 when he was 60. Mercury offers a bag of gold to Robert Morris, the "financier of the Revolution." Vulcan rests his foot on a cannon. Ceres rides a reaper and Neptune and Aphrodite, holding the Atlantic cable, rise from the sea. Minerva speaks to Benjamin Franklin, Samuel F. B. Morse and Robert Fulton. Armed Freedom, modeled by Brumidi's young wife, triumphs over Tyranny and Kingly Power.

George Washington in his Masonic regalia laid the cornerstone on September 18 in 1793, undaunted by the description of the Capitol site by one caustic observer as "a howling, malarious wilderness." The swamps have been drained, the grounds cleared and manicured. But Capitol Hill can still be buffeted by wind and snow as Maroon found out on a hike through the blizzard of 1966. He photographed the grand old matron through the swirls of snow and in his view finder, as he struggled with numbed fingers, he felt he had registered a portrait of the Capitol "clean and stark, like it had come out of one of those original paintings."

The Capitol, however, is never frozen in any time. After Washington's cornerstone laying and the ox roast that followed, the building grew with the nation. It was burned by the British in 1814, rebuilt and expanded. It housed northern regiments when the Civil War broke out. A story that endures is that one of the troopers, when shown the desk that had been used by Jefferson Davis, slashed the side with his bayonet. The desk, used by Mississippi's Senator John Stennis, has a small block of inlaid

wood presumably marking the spot. The nine-million-pound cast iron dome was completed in 1863 when they hoisted the head of the bronze sculpture of the Goddess of Freedom into place. By 1916 they had finished the East Pediment. John Kennedy took his oath of office in 1961 just at the time a new East Front had been completed. Now there are plans for a new West Front.

The Capitol represents only one part of the institutional tripod that is our government. Another, the White House, is a mile down Pennsylvania Avenue. A symbol of our greatest aspirations, the White House is home, office, power center and museum. In the mornings the tourists, sometimes as many as 15,000, stream through the state rooms on the first floor. The official business of the President and his First Lady set the rhythm. The long, black limousines slide in and out of West Executive Avenue bringing Cabinet officers and agency heads. Visiting delegations of 4-H'ers or Boy Scouts gather in the Rose Garden or on the South Lawn for short talks with the Chief Executive. Frequently the evenings are given over to dinners for visiting heads of state. But when all visitors have left, the White House becomes a home. It is the place where Abigail Adams hung her wash even before the building was finished. Thomas Jefferson had two mounds graded to add interest to his view. John Quincy Adams planted an American elm whose crown still dominates the horizon. Andrew Jackson's magnolias flank the rear door. Teddy Roosevelt built the West Wing where the President's Oval Office is located. His cousin Franklin Roosevelt built the East Wing. Each family has left its chapter in White House history.

The Supreme Court building, representing the third leg of the governmental tripod, looks out of Maroon's portrait through a frame of frozen branches and leaves. The last color of fall was caught in one of those sudden Washington storms of early December. It is fitting. The Court by design is remote, beyond the easy reach of the kind of capriciousness that sometimes infects the Capitol and the White House. The Court is the conscience in our government of laws. It has never been more evident than in these years when Court decisions have repeatedly changed our national directions. There has rarely been a more dramatic moment than in July of 1974 when Chief Justice Warren E. Burger, who was given his job by Richard Nixon, read the unanimous court decision ordering the President to yield the Watergate evidence which ultimately brought the demands for Nixon's resignation. There has been no more important decision in this century than the 1954 "Brown" decision which ordered an end to racial segregation in American schools, a convulsive affirmation of equality that is still being played out in our national life.

There has always been this kind of drama in the Supreme Court. The justices sit as "a kind of Constitutional Convention in continuous session," said Woodrow Wilson. John Quincy Adams, Henry Clay and Daniel Webster argued before the Court. One mortally ill lawyer left his hospital bed to argue his case, then died the next day. A speechless young barrister once blurted, "Mr. Chief Justice, may I have a minute to compose myself? I'm scared to death." Said Chief Justice Charles Evans Hughes in 1932 when he helped President Herbert Hoover lay the cornerstone of the new building, "The Republic endures and this is the symbol of its faith."

Before Congress, President and Supreme Court came to the Potomac River, there was a town—George-Town. Established in 1751, the tiny community of Scots grew quickly due to its location at the head of navigation on the Potomac River. George Washington once ranked it as the greatest tobacco market in Maryland and foresaw a seaport eventually rivaling Philadelphia or New York. The General passed through George-Town on the way to his first inauguration in New York. He was back in 1790 and "in company with the principal gentlemen of the town he set out to view the adjacent country in order to fix upon a future situation for 'The Grand Columbian Federal City.' " Before long Washington was conferring with Major Pierre Charles L'Enfant about plans for the Capital City while sitting in Suter's Tavern. The Washington City that we know overwhelmed and absorbed its progenitor and Georgetown today is officially nothing more than a topographical neighborhood. Yet, its poise and individualistic atmosphere and architecture have been preserved. One writer insisted that modern Georgetown has been and is the powerhouse of the free world, "the seat of the governing class." Its homes have been visited by almost every President. "The people—their homes—

are never disappointing," says photographer Maroon. He lives there so he should know.

Wherever one lives in the Capital City, one uses the Washington Monument as a visual ground zero—a basic point of geographical reference. Bathed in floodlight, the marble spike anchors the mall between the Capitol and the Lincoln Memorial. Those simple lines obscure an anguished history. Begun in 1848, it progressed 152 feet but in 1854 work halted when a marble slab from Pope Pius IX was stolen from the monument grounds and never recovered. The vandals were suspected members of the "Know-Nothing" Party, then campaigning against Catholics and foreigners. Through the Civil War the monument stood like an ugly stump in the midst of a stockyard and slaughterhouse that provided meat for Union troops. By 1876 the nation was conscience-stricken and the monument was turned over to the Army Engineers. They discovered a slight tilt and had to shore up the foundation. The faces of the monument did not align exactly with the compass and the shaft was given a modest twist. On February 21, 1885 President Chester Arthur doffed his silk hat, put aside his doeskin gloves and declared it "dedicated from this time forth to the immortal name and memory of George Washington."

There are other kinds of monuments in the mosaic of mid-Atlantic that are a gauge to our past and commentary on the present. Pittsburgh, in the western reaches of Pennsylvania, has the Golden Triangle, a portion of the central city that has been rehabilitated, giving new class to the dingy steel town. The giant chemical complexes that had their start in 1802 in Eleuthére DuPont's gun powder factory sprawl along the Brandywine at Wilmington, mingled now with the lush estates of his progeny.

Amid the smoke and bustle of Baltimore's inner harbor sits Fort McHenry. The ceremonial color guards go through their rituals oblivious to the turmoil around them. The tourists who make their way to the small enclave are almost as struck by the disintegrating city that surrounds it and the shattering blasts from the horns of the passing ships as they are by the fort. But it had its day—September 13-14, 1814. For more than 20

P 53   A boatman heads down the Severn River at Annapolis, Maryland.

Pp 54-55   The flag is still carefully tended at Fort McHenry in Baltimore's harbor, where in 1814 it flew "by the dawn's early light."

P 56   Cadets from the United States Naval Academy march through Annapolis.

P 57   Independence Hall, Philadelphia, Pennsylvania. Where the Founding Fathers began their experiment in liberty.

Pp 58-59   The Amish farm country in southeastern Pennsylvania, an island of tranquility in megalopolis.

hours the invading British poured everything they had into Fort McHenry. Eight miles away a Georgetown lawyer named Francis Scott Key was on a flag-of-truce sloop in the custody of the British, with whom he was trying to negotiate the release of an arrested friend. All day he watched the battle through a spyglass. At night the bursting shells showed that Fort McHenry had not yielded. But at 4 a.m. the bombardment ceased. With the silence came great anxiety. Grey rain clouds held back the first light. Key could see nothing through his glass until an easterly breeze cleared the morning air. Then he saw it—the American flag flying over the scarred parapets of Fort McHenry. Key took out an envelope and began writing a poem on the back. He continued writing as the small boat took him ashore in Baltimore. That poem became *The Star Spangled Banner* and was made our national anthem by act of Congress in 1931.

There is no single moment like that one to limn the history of Annapolis, Maryland's capital. Perhaps it does not need one. While Baltimore has grown and spread, Annapolis has clung tenaciously to its modest size and the graceful lines and manners of its long past. John Hanson was schooled in the early politics of Annapolis and became President under the Articles of Confederation in 1781. His descendants claim him to be the rightful holder of the title of first President of the nation. Maroon's picture is taken through the leaded glass of the Hammond-Harwood House built in 1774. A group of plebes from the United States Naval Academy are on their way to Sunday church, a custom as old as the Academy which was founded in 1845.

It was the delegates to the Second Continental Congress meeting up in Pennsylvania in 1775-1776, who gathered together all the lessons of their past and their hopes for the future and proclaimed American independence. Like so many things that had happened and would happen in the new land, the Declaration of Independence came out of the protesting minds of men both high and low. Nothing galvanized the assembly as much as *Common Sense,* the tract written by Thomas Paine, a 38-year-old, self-educated failure with an unusual fondness for the bottle. Casting off a king, he wrote, "may at first seem strange and difficult, but like all other steps which we have already passed over, will in a little time become familiar and agreeable . . . " The Declaration of Independence was more eloquent, the polished prose of Virginia's Thomas Jefferson, who drafted it in a second-story room rented from a bricklayer. The Declaration passed on July 4 and was read to the public on July 8 from the balcony of the State House. The greatest experiment in liberty that man had ever tried had begun in the modest hall pictured here. And within the next decade the determined men were fashioning another miracle in the same place. It was called the Constitution of The United States of America.

If the clatter of tourists and the whir of modern Philadelphia are nerve wracking, a cure is not far away in the countryside. "There is a strength in the land that you just cannot ignore," says Maroon who was born a city boy. He had been photographing buildings and machines when one day he went into the Amish community in southeastern Pennsylvania. The shy people seemed to recede before his lens and to blend into the land. The structures on the farms seemed planted, a part of the earth's bounty. There was simplicity and peace. "There is something special about the farmers who take from the earth, use it, but do not violate it," says Maroon. His picture is in the fall with the harvest over, the barns full and the Amish confidently ready for winter. They are at the center of a dramatic clash. The modern, industrialized and highly mobile society which science and technology have created surrounds and clamors to consume the tranquil Amish islands. They endure in their splendid isolation by the strength of Romans 12:2—"Be not conformed to this world, but be ye transformed by the renewing of your mind that ye may prove what is that good and acceptable and perfect will of God."

The men who design and build bridges link air and earth, sending their massive towers from the water into the clouds and draping them with steel cables that chain them to the land. The Delaware Memorial Bridge has such a godly profile. The twin bridges span the Delaware River and join the state to New Jersey. But for all of their stateliness they are a part of the ganglia of highways that have turned so much of mid-Atlantic into snarling, stinking raceways. They are necessary, but rarely that nice. Maroon caught the functional glory in his camera. The

New York City still is the greatest melting pot of America. Races and cultures mix; interests blend. The Metropolitan Museum of Art is shown here.

towers of the bridges rise 530 feet, the spidery cables gracefully cradling the roadbed which is 440 feet over the water. The Delaware River and Bay Authority proudly catalogued the 200 millionth vehicle in 1969 and now nearly 20 million pour across the bridges each year.

Oases of water and trees, places to breathe and think and play, have survived even under the onslaught of the automobile. Among them are college campuses. Education has nourished our system. It has pushed back the frontiers while staying rooted to traditions and fixed principles. It has spawned a special aristocracy based on ability as Thomas Jefferson foresaw. Maroon went to Princeton for his picture and found the shell crew practicing on Lake Carnegie. "There is something old and established about this scene," he says. Princeton got Lake Carnegie in 1906, a gift from philanthropist Andrew Carnegie. The university's President Woodrow Wilson would rather have had the money to raise the salaries of the professors. "As one Scot-Irish to a Scot," he said to Carnegie, "we asked for bread and you gave us cake." The undergraduates felt a little more kindly. When the 3-1/2-mile lake was dedicated after damming up Millstone River, they gave Carnegie a cheer, "Andy, Andy, you're a dandy."

Andrew Carnegie also had something to do with New York. His steel helped make the modern city, profiled in Maroon's study of Park Avenue. New York's skyline cannot be matched anyplace in the world and probably never will be. In the summer of 1974, a small Frenchman felt compelled to test himself against the twin towers of the New York World Trade Center. Philippe Petit and his friends sneaked to the top of the uncompleted buildings. With a cross bow device they fired a tightrope the 90 feet between the towers at the 110th story. In the morning Petit began his walk 1,350 feet above the street. The New Yorkers paused to pay attention and tacit tribute to this wry sign of their pre-eminence. Petit was arrested, taken off to a psychiatric clinic for study, and then pronounced quite sane. Though a little down at the heels, plagued with human, environmental and financial problems, New York can still glow with creativity. Beauty and grace on the stage are unsurpassed as shown in Maroon's picture of the New York City Ballet in a scene from the *Nutcracker Suite.* New York remains a special kingdom of the mid-Atlantic states.

NEW ENGLAND

MAINE, VERMONT,
NEW HAMPSHIRE, MASSACHUSETTS,
CONNECTICUT, RHODE ISLAND

The New England states cling tightly to their rocky, watery roots, seemingly less changed and less changing than other regions. It is an illusion of sorts. They have shared in the miracles of transportation and industry. They built the magnificent fleet of three-masted, square-rigged Yankee clippers, the greatest and fastest sailing vessels on the oceans for much of the 19th Century. When steamships put sailing vessels out of business, New England was already busy with textiles, the nation's first major manufacturing industry. America's first mill went up at Pawtucket, Rhode Island, in 1789. By 1840 some Boston merchants had changed a farming village into the first factory town and called it Lowell. The enterprise developed in the textile mills was ready and eager for new ventures like railroads and arms. So it went.

Boston's Route 128 now is a complex of industrial parks with the most sophisticated and productive electronic plants in America. And in the center of the city dozens of acres of decrepit buildings have been shoveled away to make room for new offices, hotels, apartments, arcades, convention and exhibition halls and theaters. But always there are the reminders of the past. The house of Paul Revere, 100 years old when he moved into it, nestles by the huge Government Center. One high-rise project designed by I. M. Pei, the Chinese-born architect, is on the waterfront where the Yankee clipper ships unloaded their cargoes. Author Joe McCarthy says that the State Street Bank, built by British money, is on the spot where British tea was dumped into the harbor in the great Tea Party of 1773.

The Freedom Trail, a mile and a half of history preserved and marked by Boston officials, is a route back through American heritage. The old

buildings and their stirring stories overshadow all that is around them. Not far from Paul Revere's home is the Old North Church, where lanterns were hung to warn of the British troop movements. Faneuil Hall, the "Cradle of Liberty" where the revolutionary town meetings took place, stands as dignified as ever and just as in colonial days there are produce and meat stalls on the lower floor that do a brisk business. There is a story that the famous Brinks' robbers of 1950 abandoned one plan for the burglary that called for the use of explosives out of fear that they might damage the nearby Cradle of Liberty. Along the Freedom Trail one can savor the Old Corner Book Store, looking as it did when visited by Hawthorne, Longfellow, Emerson and James Russell Lowell. John Hancock, Samuel Adams and Paul Revere lie in the Old Granary Burying Ground. There is the Boston Common, the training ground of the militia as early as 1634 and where General Howe's Britishers drilled when they were besieged by George Washington's troops during the winter of 1775-76. And then there is School Street, the former site of the Boston Latin School, the nation's first public educational institution.

Boston has always been the hub of the Yankee universe. But the modern Boston is not the encompassing mark of today's New England, at least not to the heart. Harvard and Yale mean more than urban renewal. The town meetings and the village greens that lie beyond stand out in many minds as more important than the expressways. There is something else. In the quiet valleys and tranquil towns a New England character seems to endure in proportion to its contact with the land and the weather. Historian James Thruslow Adams, writing about the New England character, put it this way: "The gristle of conscience, work, thrift, shrewdness, duty became bone."

They were frozen Puritans. Writer Jean Stafford suggests that the Pilgrims gave too much credit to God for seeing them through the first winter; their own determined endurance was one of the marvels of history. The Yankees still refer to the year 1816, when there was frost each of the 12 months and snow in July and August, as "eighteen hundred and froze to death." The long cold ("nine months of winter and three months of damn poor sleddin' ") made New Englanders place their houses together for comfort and aid as well as other reasons. For two centuries they remained an almost completely homogeneous stronghold with the same English background and the same stern religious beliefs. Not until well into the 19th Century did the waves of immigration from Europe and Canada spill over into their preserve of ocean, forest and mountain.

The towns formed around village commons. The community living fostered the town meetings, a basic ingredient of our democracy. The winters hardened the Yankee bodies but also gave them time to ponder the deeper meanings in the Bible. What was formed then still endures to a remarkable degree. More than in any other region there is a fixed character in New England.

It is like some kind of stage setting. New England lures artists to sketch its quaintness. Vacationers come to savor its vistas of sea and mountains, to sit in comfort on summer days that boil the rest of the nation. Its once dreaded snow has been turned into profit by ski resorts. New England is to look at and enjoy. The people still make paper and maple syrup, grow cranberries and potatoes. They educate a lot of our young people. But more and more they are just New Englanders, inheritors and now the preservers of something proud and beautiful in soul and in land.

The legend of courage and endurance born in the great whaling days of Nantucket lives on in its quiet streets, sensible homes and enduring patriotism.

Fred Maroon took his special journey through a New England fall, pondering the grace that comes from man in splendid harmony with his environment. He had heard the stories of the luxury of a Maine summer from his mother who had gone there as a young girl. His first stop was Acadia National Park where she had been. Before dawn he was on the crest of a rocky promontory waiting for the light. Pine and sea mingled in a deeply satisfying aroma. The powerful surge of the surf against the granite shore set the morning cadence. Birds woke and sent out their first plaintive notes. Then came the light. Dark greys thinned into blue. The water emerged and formed into an infinite black sheet. The line of distant forest became dark green. Each second the color shifted, a motion picture of the earth's endless rhythm.

Man intruded. The faint chugging of a boat's engine rose over the surf. At first the photographer resented the other's presence and then regretted his own angry thoughts. The intruder was a lobster fisherman and he belonged there more. The fisherman came into sight and his boat penciled the thin ripples across the clean tablet of water. It was complete—rock, forest, water and the man who lived off it and was in turn shaped by it.

There is trouble in the lobster industry today. Demand as well as a decline in catch has sent the price of lobsters soaring. The lobster take fell from a high of 11,000 metric tons in 1957 to 7,500 metric tons in recent years—a drop of 33 per cent. Despite the best efforts of the Maine hatcheries to raise and plant the baby lobsters, the harvest continues to decline. Lobsters are New Englanders, too, not to be sown like corn or rushed to maturity like cattle. There have been many efforts to transplant the American lobster to the Pacific Coast but none of them worked very well. The lobsters never reached commercial proportions which is one reason the 7,000 licensed lobstermen of Maine still cling in reasonable contentment to their small, weathered homes that cluster around the harbors. Maroon's picture is of Corea as the day's work of the fishermen gets underway.

Maroon went to Woodstock, Vermont, the home of naturalist George Perkins Marsh, with Lady Bird Johnson. At the time, Marsh's Victorian house, owned now by Laurance Rockefeller, had been declared a national historic landmark, one of close to 1,200 buildings, sites and monuments of designated significance. Vermont summers were made for porches like the one on the Marsh home. The white wicker furniture keeps a back straight. The view of sky and hills keeps a heart young. There is a theory held by the great fraternity of porch lovers that the fragrances of nature carried on a fresh breeze can do as much as anything to calm a person and heal the inner human wounds. More than a century ago, Marsh sat on his porch and formed the thoughts he put down in his book, *Man and Nature,* a classic treatise on conservation that started this nation thinking about its precious natural heritage. His legacy is carried on now by many like Richard Saltonstall, Jr., a Bostonian with a special passion for Maine and open land. His book, *Maine Pilgrimage,* is a latter day plea for the same spirit of renewal that Marsh urged. Saltonstall went further. He was searching for an American way of life which has been extinguished in so many regions by the ruthless march of industry and its siren call of mobility. "The concept of a family place, a house where you grew up and where you understood what your parents did and what was expected of you—all this died," he wrote. "And it was inevitable that the new generation, the young people, should rebel . . . sound value systems cannot germinate and thrive when people are concerned mainly with their material survival and when the ground is always moving out from under them . . . and this is why Maine and other rural states and regions became important points of refuge in the late sixties and early seventies. They were second frontiers where American values could, perhaps, be revived . . . The recapturing of an essential American way of life, where the family is paramount, where a person has control over his own destiny, is the inevitable next step."

The village green of Newfane, Vermont, is a way of life. Maroon's picture is at the end of a day with the golden sun streaming over the Windham County Courthouse, across thick grass and through the timeless branches of the maples. Here is a place to pause, to think, to feel good, to talk, to be happy. The darker natures of the human soul are just not welcome in such an environment. There had to be some magic ingredient in the makeup of those Yankees who paced off the town squares and raised their churches and meeting halls around them. They knew what men and women needed to bring them together with humor and goodwill.

Turning recreation into business is one way that the entrepreneurs of New England have sought to harmonize their land with their lives. Since World War II they have planted ski resorts in profusion across the mountains. Skiing is a $200 million business for the New England states. The lodges scar the mountains, true, the ungainly lifts cut through the forests. And yet the marriage of snow to the cash register is probably as easy an accommodation as man and nature can reach in these times. Snow renews itself. So do the people who use it. The late Bobby Kennedy, who used to ski the Waterville, New Hampshire, slopes that Maroon photographed, found nothing so rehabilitating. Kennedy once explained that skiing was the only sport in which he could indulge that took his mind totally off

The rich heritage of fertile land, practical traditions of yeomen and builders permeate the Connecticut River Valley. Many of the tidy towns like Sunderland, Massachusetts, are still intact.

other matters. At speeds up to 50 m.p.h. the enthusiast who lets other thoughts intrude will soon end up in the hospital. "There is something incredibly sensuous about skiing," said one participant. "Speeding down a mountain is like a narcotic." Then there is the rest, the moment to be warmed with food and good fellowship, to let weary muscles go slack and sleepy. It is this day's end sigh from the slopes of Mt. Tecumseh that we see in this book.

It is an irony that part of this valuable ski area bears the name of the old Shawnee chief who hated the white man's idea that land was to be owned and exploited by individuals. In the Indian world, land was a sacred trust of all the community, never to be subdivided and parceled out. Tecumseh in 1806 grew angry over incursions on tribal lands. "No tribe has the right to sell, even to each other, much less to strangers," he raged. "Sell a country! Why not sell the air, the great sea, as well as the earth?"

The Yankees never figured out how to sell the sea or they might have tried. No boundaries could be fixed. The sea in anger destroyed almost any man-made structure or it stealthily rotted it away with its salt. There was also its special mystery and power. It mesmerized men. It lured them and drowned them. It soothed them and excited them. The sea was not something to subdivide. Nantucket, its tidy homes festooned with American flags, with its gentle beaches and boats, has kept the love affair alive.

Perhaps nobody has described the old ways of Nantucket better than Melville. "What wonder then," he wrote in his novel of Moby Dick, the great white whale, "that these Nantucketers, born on a beach, should take to the sea for a livelihood! They first caught crabs and quahogs in the sand; grown bolder, they waded out with nets for mackerel; more experienced, they pushed off in boats and captured cod; and at last, launching a navy of great ships on the sea, explored this watery world; put an incessant belt of circumnavigations round it; peeped in at Behring's Straits; and in all seasons and all oceans declared everlasting war with the mightiest animated mass that has survived the flood; most monstrous and most mountainous! That Himmalehan, salt-sea mastodon, clothed with such portentousness of unconscious power, that his very panics are more to be dreaded than his most fearless and malicious assaults."

Mark Twain chose Hartford for his home after he had become famous. Bushnell Park, shown here, is in front of the Connecticut Capitol.

There are a few on the island who can remember the fading traces of the legend. But not many. Most of the people come in the summers from the eastern cities and they sit and stare at the water and dabble in the surf and only vaguely perceive what used to be. In 1712, Captain Christopher Hussey's sloop was blown out to sea by a fierce north wind. Riding helplessly in the Atlantic, he spotted the first school of sperm whales he had ever seen. He caught one and brought it back to Nantucket and the age of whaling began in America.

Sperm whales roamed far out to sea and they attacked their attackers. But they repaid the dangers of the chase, according to historian T. Harry Williams. Their oil shone brighter in the lamps and they yielded up from their massive heads some five tons of spermaceti from which the finest candles could be made. By 1846, some 736 American whaling ships were on the seven seas. The Essex was sunk in the Pacific by a raging 85-foot whale that "came down upon us with full speed and struck the ship with his head." A New London whaler actually stayed out of port for 11 years before returning with a full load. Winches were hooked in the blubber and it was unrolled, cut up and boiled in huge caldrons. One sperm whale could yield 2,500 gallons of oil, worth $1.49 a gallon in 1854. At its peak the whaling industry employed 17,000 men who came out of the harbors of New Bedford, Mystic, Providence and a dozen other ports.

Then came trouble. Petroleum oil was produced in quantity in 1859 and it rapidly replaced whale oil in homes and factories. During the Civil War, 70 whalers were sunk by the Confederates. In 1871, a great fleet of Arctic whalers was wrecked by ice brought in by an unexpected southwest wind. The great whaling days were over.

Not all of New England's water is salt. There are cold and crystal lakes, mountain streams and meandering rivers. The Connecticut River is New England's longest, winding 407 miles from its beginning near Quebec, down between Vermont and New Hampshire, through Massachusetts and Connecticut where it empties into Long Island Sound. It is one of the nation's most beautiful rivers. For much of its course it is contained by rugged hills, but in Massachusetts and Connecticut the land subsides into meadows and fields where onions, celery and tobacco grow. Along its way there are villages with a strong colonial flavor. "If I were a river that is where I would like to go," said photographer Maroon who followed part of its course in search of his pictures.

If there is much food for the soul in New England, there is also plenty of food for the body. And while our corn and beans and squash were adapted by New Englanders from the Indians, sea food is the staple of renown in this age. Before those first crops grew for the Pilgrims they sustained themselves on what they got from the sea. Clams crowded the mud-flats and lobsters that could feed four men could be picked up in the rocky pools along the shore. Appreciation of this bounty has grown over the years as the ease of the catch has diminished. New England has ripened its cooking traditions into the most distinctive style in the United States. President John Kennedy would not go out on Cape Cod waters on his yacht, the "Honey Fitz," until the fish chowder was finished and packed for lunch. He almost always ate two bowls. "A clambake is one of the wonders of this country," Maroon insists. "With corn roasted in its own husk, potatoes and lobster, you have the makings of an orgy the likes of which Rome never knew." True. But Newport surely has.

They still relish some of the old Yankee traditions there. Howard Gardiner Cushing, Sr., often called the Duke of Newport, carefully tends his own lobster pots. They have clambakes at such places as Land's End, once Edith Wharton's romantic house. Newport is the summer playground of 250 or so of America's superrich. It no longer has the grandeur that it had in Cornelius Vanderbilt's day (1895) when for $5 million he completed his "cottage," the Breakers, which Maroon photographed. Yet, Newport has plenty. Some of the rich people are there because other rich people are there. But the real reason for being there is the weather—the sunny, dry and comfortable warm summer—and the water. When the 12-meter yachts assemble for the America's Cup Races, the sailing duel is not half so spectacular as the spectator fleet. If America had an aristocracy in the European tradition, perhaps those who still summer in the mansions of Newport could rightly lay claim to the title. But America does not. Newport is a charming facade.

THE SOUTH

VIRGINIA, WEST VIRGINIA, NORTH CAROLINA,
SOUTH CAROLINA, GEORGIA, FLORIDA, KENTUCKY, TENNESSEE,
ALABAMA, MISSISSIPPI, LOUISIANA, ARKANSAS

The south has always been changing. Captain John Smith, the leader of America's first permanent settlement, had no expansive ideas about slavery. He worked desperately just to survive. But half a century before Jamestown took root on its river bank the Spanish adventurers had brought slaves to the New World and the institution was growing and soon would overwhelm the whole region. It was almost a natural phenomenon. Southern agriculture—tobacco, corn, rice, cotton—was dull, hard work requiring large unskilled labor forces. The landholders assumed slaves were necessary equipment and by 1730 South Carolina had two slaves for every white person. Within 200 years of the day when Captain Smith dropped anchor and decided to stay, slavery was flourishing from Virginia west to the Mississippi River.

Then as society matured the doubts about slavery that men had held within themselves emerged. The Civil War ended it, but not its legacy of segregation. Rebuilding and rethinking went on for two more generations until after World War II. Northern industry, lured by climate, labor and land, started moving south while 4.5 million blacks went north to megalopolis, enticed by welfare checks and the job market. Those who stayed behind began to assert themselves, demand true equality; and in 1954, the Supreme Court said the whites must begin to give it to them. The civil rights convulsion of the 1960's shook southern social foundations. Meantime, white retirees from Chicago and New York flocked to the salubrious climes of Florida, South Carolina and Georgia. With new will and new wealth, some southern cities integrated their schools better than their northern counterparts who preached but did not practice the justice

P 93   Mount Vernon, a reflection of George Washington's sense of place and purpose.

Pp 94-95   Monticello, with grace and meaning out of the life of Thomas Jefferson.

Pp 96-97   Williamsburg, Virginia. Christmas Fifes and Drums ceremony.

P 98   North Fork, West Virginia, forgotten coal town.

P 99   Coal trains of Williamson, West Virginia.

Pp 100-101   Edenton, North Carolina, where southern legend is nurtured.

of the Constitution. Now there is more change. Some blacks, having rubbed together in northern ghettos, their dreams of instant prosperity and equality diminished, are trickling back. Others who have been educated and trained have felt a call to return. Industry continues to move into the uncrowded and warm latitudes where workers can live just down the road. There is the energy equivalent of two Middle Easts in the coal of West Virginia alone, a resource whose value cannot be estimated in this power hungry world. Florida boasts nearly three million head of cattle and the south's yield from 14 million acres of cotton planted each year is worth four billion dollars.

Today the south is the honey pot. It is growing faster, says the Bureau of the Census, than any other region of America. The sociologists, psephologists, city planners and land use specialists are flocking south, putting the people and the places under the microscope. It is a fascinating human and geographical drama with no predictable climax in no predictable year.

Whatever emerges it is almost a certainty that the inner anguish and toil which creates the south of the future will be documented with deep feeling by its own historians, poets, writers, playwrights and journalists. Since World War I the region has produced far more than its share of this talent. Thomas Wolfe, William Faulkner, Erskine Caldwell, Robert Penn Warren, Douglas Southall Freeman, Tennessee Williams, Harper Lee, Richard Wright. The names march out in a colorful procession. They won so many awards and prizes as their plays and novels crowded into America's creative currents that the southern writers' heritage became a subject of analysis itself. These southern story tellers were all influenced by the Bible, absorbing its beauty and mysticism in varying degrees. They were infused with the deep sense of trauma the Civil War brought their land. They also seemed to inherit a joy of language well used. Faulkner, the Nobel Prize winner, described the south as "opaque, slow, violent, shaping and creating the life of man in its implacable and brooding image."

The south is a great moiling land mass that in photographer Maroon's viewfinder runs 1,200 miles from east to west and a thousand miles from that far tip of Florida to the top of the Virginias. There is no common life style. There is, however, history and tradition. They are the texture

The middle ground between Maine and Florida is Hilton Head, South Carolina. Winters are mild, summers too. Year-round pleasure is part of the package.

of the south. They shade the manners of the people and gently guide its greater aspirations. Mount Vernon, George Washington's beloved home, comes first. It is planted there firmly on its magnificent hilltop that scans the Potomac River. It is a state of mind as much as anything, still calling out for excellence and determination. "You can read a person," says Maroon, "by his buildings." There are, broadly speaking, two types of men in this world: the adventurers, those nomads whose only true loyalty is to the next horizon; and the homebodies, who like to sink roots and feel the familiar. Washington was the latter. He was away from home for years as Commander-in-Chief of the American Revolutionary Army but he never relished that existence. "I should enjoy more real happiness in one month with you at home," he wrote his wife before his great adventure, "than I have the most distant prospect of finding abroad, if my stay were to be seven times seven years." This quiet conservatism, so apparent in the aura of Mount Vernon, was what brought the foundling republic to strength after the tumultuous years of the Revolution.

There is a subtle difference in Monticello, the home of Thomas Jefferson. Here is the same love of the land, the appreciation of grace, the courtly setting. There is also revealed a restless mind tinkering with every conceivable gadget to improve its function, an eye that looks beyond the mountains to the far Pacific. There is wonder about the stars and the delight of developing new flowers and crops. There is, too, a quest for perfection in the affairs of man himself. A contemporary said of Jefferson that he "could calculate an eclipse, survey an estate, tie an artery, plan an edifice, try a cause, break a horse, dance the minuet, and play the violin." John Kennedy stood up one night in the White House before the Nobel Prize winners of the Western Hemisphere and toasted: "I think this is the most extraordinary collection of talent . . . that has ever been gathered together at the White House, with the possible exception of when Thomas Jefferson dined alone."

A hundred miles or so down the road is Colonial Williamsburg, the old Virginia capital in which the ideas for our nation were honed. The ghosts of Washington and Jefferson walk there. So do others. George Wythe, the lawyer who tutored Jefferson, lives in memory. The cries of Patrick

Henry for liberty seem to echo through the streets. Williamsburg, re-created by Rockefeller money is a bit romanticized, but splendidly so. Beyond the legends of the men are other things. The spell of Williamsburg is a visual thing. The sunlight touching the high tips of the old maples in the quiet of early morning. Wide streets. Brick paths between boxwood hedges. Wood piles. Benches for rest and thought. The authority of picket fences. The cozy openness. The close separateness. It forms an aura of thought and care, of collective pursuit of excellence in material, manner and mind.

There is little of this feeling in North Fork, West Virginia, a coal town that flourished, died and may come back. Maroon's camera caught it at low ebb. Dispirited. Dirty. Without hope. He prowled the grimy hills and the rail yards with the filled cars standing ready to roll. Maybe that will change. Coal is once again in demand. West Virginia's Senator Robert Byrd projects that the industry will be required to increase its output 2-1/2 times to 1.5 billion tons a year, in the next decade. Coal prosperity, however, still extracts a fearful toll from the land. Strip mining, which accounts for half of the coal produced, has taken off the natural land cover and left a devastation that may take centuries to heal. The battle between conservationists, who want more restrictions, and the coal operators goes on. But today's battles are not like the old ones. For ten years in the early part of this century a shooting war ranged in West Virginia between miners, who rose against coal operators and their allies, the sheriffs and state militia. The issue was the right of miners to join a union. It was counted as the most violent episode of civil strife and armed insurrection that this nation had seen since the Civil War. It ended only when U.S. Army infantry units supported by bombers moved into the area.

They have not forgotten the man who made the coal miner's life bearable finally. He was John L. Lewis, perhaps the most colorful of the union leaders. He rides those coal cars in memory. He is in the shafts and on the strips. He led the battles for decent wages and hours, for hospitals and vacations. He did it with mind and courage and the voice of a lion.

"I have never faltered or failed to present the cause or plead the case of the mine workers of this country," he once told his following. "I have pleaded your case not in the quavering tones of a mendicant asking alms, but in the thundering voice of the captain of a mighty host, demanding the rights to which free men are entitled."

His miners followed such entreaties with joy and fervor. When he wanted mines shut down, the pits were deserted. When he called for three-day weeks to show his muscle, that is what happened overnight. The old men, sick and dying from black lung and decades of neglect, wept openly as they were carried into the new hospitals that Lewis had the United Mine Workers build for them.

There is an emotional southern undertow. Fred Maroon felt it when he spent a boyhood year in Edenton, North Carolina, a gently decayed town on Albemarle Sound. He played in the yards of the stately old homes, swam along the waterfront. One of novelist Inglis Fletcher's characters talked about Edenton's early days: "The soft breeze off the water was pleasant; the shadows of the shore, pierced by fireflies' lamps, drew me . . . soft voices of women, sitting in the galleries, behind the vines of Jasmine and Honeysuckle; the heavy voices of men answering; men on fine horses riding down the street, followed by Negro grooms carrying lanthorns; the post lights at the cross streets, and the village green. The moon rising, almost at the full, fell on cypress trees standing deep in the dark water."

Cold and crowded northerners are re-discovering this southern allure. Those who do not like the towers of pleasure that line the Florida coast seek such way-stations in between as Charleston, South Carolina. Their migrations may ruin the older, muted places but not yet. Charleston clings to its dignity fiercely. It was once the reigning belle of colonial America. Maroon pictured the 140-year-old St. Philip's Church structure which presides quietly at the center of the city. St. Philip's was founded in 1681 close to the same time as "Charles Town." The church building now standing is the third one. George Washington worshiped at the second St. Philip's. John Wesley, the father of Methodism, preached there. And Boston's John Quincy Adams told in his journal how surprised he was that the sermon was only 20 minutes long.

The grace of the old south has been preserved in many of the antebellum homes carefully restored, like the Rosemont Plantation house, Forkland, Alabama.

Maroon believes that in graveyards one can often take the measure of a place and its people. "They say a lot about those who are still around, the appreciation for others' lives." St. Philip's goes on vigorously with a congregation of 1,300 worshiping in the midst of those who went before. Edward Rutledge, who signed the Declaration of Independence, is buried there. So is John C. Calhoun, the fiery Secretary of War and Vice President of the United States.

Atlanta is a cousin of Charleston—but distant. Atlanta is the south's biggest and richest city. She was never rooted fully in the old traditions which must account for her modern ways. Founded in 1845 at the juncture of two rail lines, Atlanta was not much more than a brash town during the Civil War. She got a little southern affection when General William T. Sherman burned the city in 1864 and thereby provided a legend for Margaret Mitchell's novel, *Gone With the Wind*. But Atlanta rebuilt hurriedly after the war, unabashedly collaborated with Yankee carpetbaggers and plunged realistically into the future. Its spirit has not dimmed. In eight years in the 1960's the entrepreneurs of Atlanta put up more than a billion dollars worth of new buildings. Of the nation's 500 largest corporations, about 400 of them are represented in Atlanta, sometimes called the New York corporate farm club. The pride of Atlantans focuses on Peach Tree Center, a complex of stores, hotels and office buildings that rivals any in the United States in design and functional grace.

The coast of Florida is another story. The battle for grace has been lost there. Huge private complexes like the Jockey Club, shown here, are the new rage for those who want to indulge their senses. Since 1970, Florida has surpassed California as the state with the largest population increase, up nearly 900,000 people. Not everything in Florida is manmade and up for sale by a long shot. But the struggle to preserve nature areas is intense. The large and aggressive Florida Audubon Society claims credit for registering four million acres of beach, swamp and forest. Maroon's picture of a blue heron in Wakulla Springs is a classic study of how the area looked when civilization stopped at Jacksonville not too many decades ago. Here is the misty early light that Maroon loves ("the time of poetry"), a willing subject for his lens, the rising song tide of birds and the chatter of small creatures, and now and then a ripple from a submerged alligator. Simple. Timeless. A moment of pure elation for a sensitive soul.

Andrew Jackson surely knew poetic moments growing up on the frontier. He knew danger too, though little of the rough and tumble of his early years is reflected in the grand style of his beloved Hermitage near Nashville. Lawyer, senator, land speculator, horse breeder, judge and general, Jackson left his mark on the west—and the United States. His election to the Presidency in 1828 was a turning point in our political history. He was the first President from west of the Appalachians, the first to be elected by direct appeal to the mass of voters and not through the manipulations of a recognized political organization. He was more beneficiary than molder of the new tide of political democracy. But his restless and impetuous spirit nudged it along and in plain, tough language made it understandable to almost everybody.

The love of fine horses has been a passion of the south from the first days. It flourishes in the border areas where climate and soil yield the bluegrass that is so nourishing for the thoroughbreds. The rolling country around Lexington, Kentucky, which has been neatly fenced into great horse farms is a special kind of monument to this love. Animals, men and the outdoors blend in a cycle of breeding, training and racing. The horses themselves share the exhilaration of their special existence and purpose. The love of running is so strong in thoroughbreds that they begin to race after their mothers when only a few hours old.

It is not far from Lexington to Cades Cove in the Great Smoky Mountains. Getting there, however, is another matter. "You see huge neon signs melt together into one illegible mess above the endless collection of souvenir shops, restaurants, motels and other tourist traps," remembers Maroon. Yet once inside the Great Smoky Mountains National Park all of that falls away. In the midst of the park is Cades Cove, a meadowland five miles long and two miles wide, a tiny preserve of life and land as it was when the first settlers found it. The old log and clapboard houses still stand. The split rail fences are carefully repaired. The fields are farmed under the watchful eyes of Park Rangers. That special patch of earth still yields a great bounty. In earlier times it was all anybody could want.

P 115   The Hermitage, beloved home of Andrew Jackson, Tennessee.

Pp 116-117   The Great Smoky Mountains, Tennessee.

P 118   Cades Cove, The Great Smoky Mountains National Park, Tennessee.

P 119   Dawn battlefield. Shiloh, Tennessee.

Pp 120-121   Cotton fields, as they were and are. Alabama.

Pp 122-123   Downtown. Holly Springs, Mississippi.

There were deer, wild turkey, raccoon, bear, mink, squirrel and rabbit. The farmers heated their homes with the huge fireplaces, slept in feather beds, forged iron and put up vegetables and fruit for the winters.

It is a continuing curiosity of our history that out of the concern for freedom and dignity of the human soul this nation's men and women fought one of the bloodiest wars of all history among themselves. "How fragile we are," thought Maroon as he prepared to take the picture of the Shiloh Battlefield in Tennessee. Twenty-three thousand men died there in 1862. The Confederate forces fell on the sleeping Union troops in the first light of April 6, about the hour that this picture was taken. Even as it reeled back, U. S. Grant's army began to patch itself together. Brigadier General Stephen Hurlbut's 4th Division held a small grove of blooming peach trees. For almost seven hours the southerners threw assault after assault against them. By evening, after horrible slaughter, the Union forces had lost the orchard, the dead bodies of both sides sprinkled with peach blossoms. Slowly, the Confederate assault ground down. The next day fresh northern forces under Major General D. C. Buell arrived and carried the field for the Union. Grant remembered the battlefield "so covered with dead that it would have been possible to walk across the clearing . . . stepping on dead bodies without a foot touching the ground."

The old south lives on in places other than parks and monuments and restored homes. There are blacks who live in shacks and pick cotton by hand and Maroon's contemporary photograph in Alabama looks more like it might have been taken by Matthew Brady a hundred years ago. But it is there, now, mid-day, hot and the work goes on. Yet, there is something new. There is hope even for the most humble tenant farmer. It was won in the brutal civil rights battles of the 1950's and 1960's. There was death and fear all across the south as the courts struck down the elaborate facades of segregation in schools, hotels and restaurants and the black leaders called up their people to walk into the forbidden territories.

There were freedom riders in 1961. There were sit-ins and exhortations from church pulpits. Four small children died in the bombing of a Birmingham church in 1963. White activists from the north were gunned down in the sultry nights with no warning. Lester Maddox rose to fame and the Governorship of Georgia with his axe handle, a symbol of his resistance to integration. Birmingham's Police Chief Bull Connor and his police dogs and water hoses were emblazoned across the world's newspapers. But to match them were James Meredith who went under guard into the University of Mississippi, the institution's first black student. And there was Martin Luther King, who preached his dream and marched with his people, then died from an assassin's bullet, but not before he had won the Nobel Prize for peace.

His caravan marches on and it is still difficult. But the momentum is there. All across the south, indeed the United States, there are growing numbers of black businessmen, civic leaders, mayors, sheriffs; and in Congress they have their own black caucus.

Back when cotton was truly king in the south, none of this could even have been imagined. Much of the beauty and tradition was built on the sweat of the black man. As in Holly Springs, a splendid little city in Marshall County, Mississippi. More cotton was produced there between 1850 and 1860 than any place else in the world. It was shipped down the Mississippi and on to the eastern United States and Europe. The money flowed back in and the wealthy men of Holly Springs built themselves magnificent homes, 75 of which still stand. Craftsmen from Europe were imported to execute the architectural details. The proud citizens of Holly Springs called their creation the "Athens of the South."

There is no celebration in the United States that equals New Orleans' Mardi Gras, where young and old join in fun and feasting in the streets of the old city.

That pride endures. When Maroon came through with his camera, the gracious matrons of the historical society furnished a baby-sitter for his children and drove him and his wife around to view the restorations. But the thing that held his interest most, even amidst all that history, was the Holly Springs bus stop, an important part of that other world that makes the mansions possible. Maroon watched most of a morning behind his long lens. No bus ever came but a lot of people acted on that small stage. Working people. Humble people. Mostly black. They moved quietly in and out of each other's lives, giving their "good mornings" and exchanging chit-chat or just sitting, in a social ritual that no doubt has been a part of Holly Springs since it was incorporated in 1837.

On down the river is a kind of southern vortex—New Orleans. It is black music and French food. It is Mardi Gras and football. It is ocean-going ships in deep harbor and a sunrise through the masts of the shrimp boats which Maroon found beyond the mouth of the Mississippi River. In another of his shots, the Joseph Clark Eureka Brass Band poses in the St. Louis Cemetery No. 2. Later that day they let him follow them in a real funeral procession. They marched to the burial with deeply moving dirges. They led the procession back to town with the riotous strains of *When the Saints Go Marching In.* It all started in the 18th Century when the French allowed the slaves to bury their dead with music. The greats of jazz like Louis Armstrong listened and learned from this tradition. Armstrong once remarked that the funeral marches "would just touch your heart, they were so beautiful."

The New Orleans mornings are for other uses as the pictures show. In one scene the light filters through the Spanish moss of Audubon Park as a horsewoman rides in graceful solitude. The bayou where Andrew Bell was fishing is not so tidy as Audubon Park but perhaps it is just as enjoyable. Bell, a descendant of a slave, seemed magnificently contented.

In the same way jazz lifts the spirits of the people of New Orleans, country music sustains the mountain people from West Virginia to Arkansas. In the kitchen of the Morrison family in Fox, Arkansas, Maroon took the picture of daughter Kathy doing a spontaneous jig. Three generations of Morrisons were there. After dinner they nestled their fiddles on their arms, grasped the bows several inches up from the handles and sawed out the old tunes with remarkable delicacy. "They turned each other on," says Maroon. "They sensed when to come in, when to stop. The music came from inside." Its special pleasure was written in their faces.

And the same simple joy of life and sharing was easy to detect in the young couple whom Maroon photographed swinging on a rope into a creek near Mountain View, Arkansas. They were far away geographically and intellectually from much of America but their smooth, youthful bodies, their laughter and their exuberance sounded a note that can be heard in every corner of the nation.

LAKE STATES

INDIANA,
ILLINOIS, OHIO, WISCONSIN,
MICHIGAN, MINNESOTA

The taproot of America goes down some place around the Great Lakes. It is sustained by the iron ore of Duluth, the blanket of loam that yields up the soybeans near Galesburg and the basin of fresh water that cleanses and nourishes the human habitations. The region is the core of this nation. The raw work is done there. The ore is turned into steel and the steel into machines. The ground is tilled and planted and the grain fed to livestock. The forests are mashed into pulp which becomes paper. Men still sweat. Women rise in the dawn to cook. It roars and stinks in places but elsewhere it is gentle and comforting. It is a child's book of factories and farms—planes, trains, trucks, automobiles, bulldozers, too.

It is as large as France but with industrial muscle exceeding that of both France and Great Britain, writer Robert McLaughlin calculated. Along the lakes is a thousand-mile belt of mills, refineries, blast furnaces and machine-tool plants. Around Chicago, a fingernail in our vast expanse, they pour more steel than in all of France. Detroit builds a third of the nation's cars and trucks. Elkhart, Indiana, makes 50 per cent of the world's band instruments. Greater Peoria, Illinois, alone has 360 factories making nearly 1,000 products. And they send it out to others in a spectacle of transportation that surpasses any other in the world. The endless threads of trains cry off into the flat nights. The jets roar out of Chicago's O'Hare, the busiest airport in the world. Barges nudged by the blocky towboats ply the inland rivers and waterways. Tankers and freighters reach the ocean with ease along the Great Lakes and the St. Lawrence Seaway. Fleets of huge trucks that leave miniature tornadoes in their wakes rumble over the freeways. There are no real mountains, but there are

shores. The state of Michigan, without touching an ocean, has the second longest (after Alaska) shoreline in the United States. There are many who insist that only here do we find the real America. In its 40 million people flows the blood of almost every nation and race on earth. The language is an homogenized product out of twang, drawl, lisp and boom.

Its sons and daughters have a curious habit of marching off to other parts of the country. They become politicians out of an abiding zeal for reform that was handed down by their ancestors. The voice of the midwest, said President Woodrow Wilson, "is a voice of protest." Yet, those who go away never forget. Some come back for nourishment, or even permanently after the wanderlust dies. Those who stay on are buffeted by severe winters and scorching summers but the worse it gets the more serene they seem to be. Perhaps man needs a struggle. Contending with the weather, with the earth, with machines may be what it is all about.

The variety of activity is staggering, as is the variety of thought. Senator Joseph McCarthy and Senator "Fighting Bob" LaFollette came from there, men so far apart politically and emotionally that it is hard to put them both within the boundaries of Wisconsin. The great liberal spokesman Clarence Darrow came out of these lands. But so did the Chicago *Tribune's* Colonel Robert R. McCormick. Chicago birthed the Rotary International, an organization of hail fellows still well met.

It is the land of hearth and homes, reveling in nostalgia and religion. Every year the Chicago *Tribune* reprints the two-panel cartoon by John T. McCutcheon called *Injun Summer,* showing an old man and a young boy beneath an autumn moon watching a field of corn shocks turn to Indian teepees and dancing braves. "Jever notice how the leaves turn red 'bout this time o'year?" the old man asks. "That's when an old Injun sperrit gits tired dancin' an' goes up and squats on a leaf t' rest . . . an' ever' once'n a while a leaf gives way under some fat old Injun ghost and comes floatin' down to the ground. See—here's one now. See how red it is? That's the war paint rubbed off'n an Injun ghost, sure's you're born." Memories of leaf bonfires and harvest moons and warm kitchens make the heart ache.

The North got three of its most successful Civil War generals from the lake states—Ulysses S. Grant, William T. Sherman and Philip Sheridan. The Confederacy borrowed its national anthem, "Dixie," from Daniel Decatur Emmett of Ohio who wrote the piece for a minstrel show. Writer McLaughlin insists that historian Charles Beard went back to Indiana one time and explained Marxism to his father, a banker, who replied: "Yes, yes, I follow you. The workers rise and take over the property. Now what I want to know is how soon do the smarties get it back?"

Johnny Appleseed roamed the region in a myth that still endures. The truth is there was a fellow named John Chapman who came from Massachusetts. He helped some of the pioneer families start orchards by selling them tiny trees from his wilderness orchards. The region is the dairyland of the nation, even though the number of people in the business continues to decline. Four of the states are among the top producers of cheese, milk and other dairy products. The dairy farms that remain are computerized and mechanized beyond any pioneer imaginings.

The full fury of the mouth of a blast furnace is both terrifying and beautiful. Making steel takes a toll of men and land and air.

It would be misleading not to point out that from the lake states came Al Capone, the king of the Chicago underworld who just may be the most famous big-time criminal of all. Close behind comes John Dillinger, robber, gunman and ladies' man, who frustrated the law until 1934 when he was shot down by FBI agents in his homeland of Chicago.

There was John Deere who made his famous plows and Cyrus McCormick with his reapers. Clem Studebaker's wagons hauled supplies for the Union Army in the Civil War. They say he helped welcome the first train into Indianapolis. And then he helped build one of the first automobiles in 1898. George M. Pullman got the idea for railroad cars that you could sleep in. His genius for innovation in mechanical ways, however, failed to carry over into human considerations. The Pullman strike of 1894, long and bloody and famous, aroused the nation to the problems between labor and management that were to mature in the next decades.

From the lake states came a certain mark in literature and learning. William McGuffey wrote his readers. General Lew Wallace authored *Ben Hur*. Strangely, Tarzan swung out of the cornfields through the pen of Edgar Rice Burroughs. There were James Whitcomb Riley and Booth Tarkington. The names go on—Theodore Dreiser, Thorstein Veblen,

John Dos Passos, Sherwood Anderson, Ernest Hemingway, Edgar Lee Masters and, of course, Carl Sandburg. It was in the 1920's that the great Baltimore iconoclast, H. L. Mencken, confessed that America's top contemporary authors came "from the Middle Empire that has Chicago for its capital." Sandburg explained:

The prairie sings to me in the forenoon and I know
in the night I rest easy in the prairie arms,
on the prairie heart.

They play basketball and football in the lake states more than they do anyplace else. They eat corn on the cob and hundreds of thousands of people come to see the roaring Indianapolis 500, America's best known auto race. They boat and canoe on the water, liquid or solid, and they hike in droves and camp by the legion in a never-ending love affair with their rich land.

In the gutsy days of Chicago, Sandburg called the city "hog butcher to the world." It isn't that anymore. They have shut down the stockyards, gone west. But the legend of hustle goes on in other places, in other effort. Fred Maroon was in Hammond, Indiana, one day to photograph a refinery. His picture shows this caldron burning, belching. Another time in Cleveland he saw and smelled and felt a blast furnace's orange mouth spit out the molten metal. Grit and heat seeped into his bones, seared his insides. How could men keep at that work, he wondered. Then he began to understand what a toll our civilization has taken not only in land and minerals, but men. The greatest problem of the future for this nation may be focused in the lake states. We cannot continue to feed that immense industrial maw as in the past. Somehow, resources, environment and man's needs must be brought into balance. If anybody can do it, these midwesterners can. They are the engineers and managers of the United States, they are the people in the boiler room who can control the rate of our national combustion.

When everything is said and written the greatest resource of this region is the people. Inventive, tough, compassionate, determined, kindly, poetic. Born of the land, nurtured in neighborliness, matured in curiosity and ambition. The airplane and the automobile were almost natural outgrowths of these traits. So were the typewriter, the cash register, the sousaphone, the carpet sweeper, the wire fly swatter, the beer can and floating soap. Writer Louis Bromfield experimented with conservation on his Ohio farm. Illinois Governor Adlai Stevenson, who ran twice for the Presidency, left his legacy of language and heartland wisdom. "I have Bloomington to thank for the most important lesson I have ever learned," he said, "that in quiet places, reason abounds; that in quiet people there is vision and purpose; that many things are revealed to the humble that are hidden from the great. I hope and pray that I can remember the great truths that seem so obvious in Bloomington but so obscure in other places." Common sense comes with the harvest. Decency is born along the shaded streets.

Maroon's picture in rural Indiana shows a deserted farm house, a casualty of technology and competition. Fifty years ago a family could live fully and comfortably on 80 acres. Today's farm in the lake states averages more than 200 acres and is growing. What was lost when this family was forced to move from this farm? There is no measure. What is it worth to a man to be his own master from dawn to dark? How can one put a price on the glories of a sunset or the deep satisfaction that comes when the crops are in and families are close around? The deserted farm is one of the scars of the heartland, as profound as any made in the earth.

The heartland gave this country its greatest leader—Abraham Lincoln. He kept us whole. He gave us back our soul and raised the aspirations of the world. His modest home has been restored in Springfield. He always wanted to go back there after being President and practice law again among the people he loved. He had a hard time leaving in the year 1861 to go east to the White House and begin his stewardship. He stood on the train's rear platform on a cold and drizzly February morning. His manner and face were melancholy. "My friends," he told the small crowd, "no one, not in my situation, can appreciate my feeling of sadness at this parting. To this place, and the kindness of these people I owe everything. Here I have lived a quarter of a century, and have passed from a young to an old man. Here my children have been born, and one buried. I now leave, not knowing when, or whether ever, I may

return, with a task before me greater than that which rested upon Washington."

Lincoln had been nominated in 1860 in Chicago, a raw town of uncertain future. Maroon's picture is of the heart of the city now, the twin cylindrical towers of Marina City rising over the Chicago River, which became one of the few rivers to be turned around when early Chicagoans decided it should flow out of the lake, not into it. By all rights there never should have been a city there. It began as a swamp. An early bank would not loan money to the tiny village, declaring it nothing more than a muddy bog. Some said the Chicago River was too shallow for boats and the streets of the village too bottomless for wagons. Chicagoans simply raised their city on stilts above the floods of the river and the lake and went on growing. Eastern experts were always writing Chicago off. Chicago always declined the honor. After the Great Fire of 1871 poet John Greenleaf Whittier lamented, "The city of the west is dead." One Chicagoan raised a sign in rebuttal: "All gone but wife, children and energy." They rebuilt the city and today it is second in size in the nation, 14th in the world, and the Sears building is the world's tallest, one of several impressive structures that give Chicago a skyline surpassed in visual impact only by the massed towers of New York.

Cleveland cannot match that. Cleveland is—well, Cleveland. She is too grimy to be called beautiful, too dilapidated to be called modern, too modern to be called quaint, too gutsy to be called dead. Maroon went to Shaker Heights for a picture of an American suburban street that has bridged old and new. Big blocky houses oozing comfort. Porches and pantries. The giant trees cast their spell over them. The kids that grew up there played in each other's back yards, went to school together, courted each other and then brought the grandchildren back home. Hear the supper calls and the trumpet practice, the old radio tuned in for the next fight of heavyweight Joe Louis.

If the Great Lakes set the character of the region, the thousands of smaller lakes give it flavor. They are people size. They break up the table top of land. They are molten silver drops that welcome canoes and sailboats and those who want to walk the shores and breathe. There are 8,000 lakes in Wisconsin, at least another 15,000 in Minnesota. Maroon's picture in the Audubon preserve in Sarona, Wisconsin, was taken in the evening as the heat ebbed and the fish began to rise again to the surface of the water and the canoeists stroked happily into the dusk. Each year more people come. They hurry from the city ovens, seeking out some sense of renewal among the lakes and marshlands. "Wilderness is the material out of which man has hammered the artifact called civilization," wrote Aldo Leopold, one of our great conservationists, in *A Sand County Almanac.* Much of his inspiration came from the days at his Wisconsin cabin. He used words with an exciting beauty that moved millions of readers to join his cause of preservation: "A dawn wind stirs on the great marsh. With almost imperceptible slowness it rolls a bank of fog across the wide morass. Like the white ghost of a glacier the mists advance, riding over phalanxes of tamarack, sliding across the bogmeadows heavy with dew. A single silence hangs from horizon to horizon."

Silence is not the staple of Detroit. It is a clangorous place, a melding of men and machine tools, steel and electronics. The rhythm of production reaches into every crevice of the area including a Saturday afternoon on Lake St. Clair captured by Maroon's camera. Out on the lake an ore boat churns toward a landing with its cargo. In the foreground the privileged people of Grosse Pointe, one of Detroit's most exclusive suburbs, sail their boats in the snappy breeze.

Even behind the elegant hedges in the great houses that wealth has made possible, the men and women rarely drift too far from the fundamentals of manufacturing. Henry Ford II, who rejuvenated the company his grandfather founded, was once described as looking and acting like a machine operator with a beer belly. The first Henry Ford, despite his countless millions, would never budge from Dearborn, where he was born and reared. His life was always enmeshed with engines and wheels. He built his own gasoline engine, then a car, started the company in 1903 with assets of $14,500, which fell to $223.65 within 24 days. In 20 years, his firm was making an annual profit of $93 million.

And evermore the automobile dominated our lives. It sent us across the

Ferris wheels at the Minnesota State Fair, St. Paul, spin through a summer night, a harvest ritual almost as old as the farm society that still is the strength of this land.

country in search of markets, new sights and pleasures; it shaped our cities, spawned the suburbs, and brought the modern shopping center. Maroon's picture is of one of the new shopping malls in Minneapolis. Stores, shops, restaurants and the central plaza are totally enclosed. Heated in the winter, air conditioned in the summer, the shopper need be buffeted by the elements only in the short dash from auto to entrance. The chroniclers of merchandising suggest that the idea of the shopping center goes back to the 15th Century when in Nizhni Novgorod, now the Soviet Union's city of Gorki, merchants attending the trading fair decided to have permanent buildings and bazaars. The small towns of the lake states with their court house squares used some of the same idea. The stores which formed the square often had awnings or roofs that covered the walk in front. Their patrons could window browse around the square, protected from sun, rain and snow. One of the first modern shopping centers was the Country Club Plaza of Kansas City, Missouri, built in the twenties. After World War II as the streets and parking areas of the central cities filled up to bursting, the merchants rushed to the outlying areas where the people were moving and where there was land for parking aprons around the stores. In 25 years, 15,000 shopping centers were built in the United States. The most spectacular in 1974 was the world's largest enclosed shopping center at Schaumburg, Illinois, near O'Hare airport. On 191 acres of land organized by Mayor Bob Atcher, the Woodfield Center is a multi-level collection of huge branch department stores like Marshall Field and J. C. Penney and some 200 smaller stores. It is a seven-day-a-week operation which boasts a Sunday "champagne brunch" in the Seven Arches Restaurant, one of more than 30 eating places.

There will undoubtedly be bigger and better shopping centers in the heartland before many more years go by. There will be bigger and better everything and the people who live around the Great Lakes will be the vital element in this future. Some years ago Senator Everett Dirksen, who came from the small Illinois town of Pekin, pondered the men and women of the lake states. "Hopelessness is alien," he wrote. "They work and persevere and then they work some more. Vitality is everywhere—a people who are a little less than the angels but always trying to do better."

THE PLAINS

IOWA, MISSOURI,
OKLAHOMA, KANSAS, NEBRASKA, SOUTH DAKOTA,
NORTH DAKOTA, TEXAS

One's mind labors to rebuild the world as it must have been on the morning of July 30, 1804, for William Clark. He scuffed through the prairie grass, up the Missouri River bluffs near where Omaha would be and then he stood in the wind and looked out over America's land ocean.

The Virginian was a man of distinguished intelligence, great sensitivity and inventiveness, as was the expedition's other leader, Meriwether Lewis. Clark understood as well as anyone the richness and potential of the raw territory which they were exploring. Clark had lived in the wilderness, fought in it, loved it. And on that morning even he was awed by what spread out before him. The emotion stayed with him until the evening when he was back down near the Missouri and writing in the log. Some of the feeling found its way into what was normally a very calm and scientific chronicle of one of man's greatest explorations.

"Lewis & (I) went up the Bank and walked a Short Distance in the high Prairie," he wrote. "This Prairie is Covered with Grass of 10 or 12 inches in hight, Soil of good quality & at the Distance of about a mile further back the Countrey rises about 80 or 90 feet higher, and is one Continued Plain as fur as Can be seen, from the Bluff on the 2d rise immediately above our Camp, the most butifull Plains, interspursed with Groves of timber, and each point Covered with tall timber . . ."

No fences, or buildings, or highways or homes. Most likely great summer clouds sculptured in a deep blue, rising in ranks over the endless land. Rich. Serene. Almost a dream. Lonely, too. Frightening in its vastness.

Plains Indians, after they got their horses from the exploring Spaniards of the 1500's, had experienced this great force of space and land and sky.

P 155 Iowa corn in the crib.

Pp 156-157 Steel rails conquered the land ocean. The afternoon sun glints off the train yards in Kansas City, Missouri.

Pp 158-159 Gateway Arch, St. Louis, Missouri. Many of those who explored and settled the west began their journeys on the riverfront where the Arch now stands.

Pp 160-161 An Indian village, Tsa-la-gi, Oklahoma. Conquered, maltreated, neglected. Indians now struggle to preserve their heritage.

P 162 Symbols of productive might, grain elevators near Dodge City, Kansas, rise boldly on the endless horizon, the prairie's answer to New York's skyscrapers.

William Brandon, an authority on Plains Indians, wrote about it. "Above all the new world of the horse brought time and temptation to dream. The plains are afloat in mysterious space, and the winds come straight from heaven. Anyone alone in the plains turns into a mystic. The plains had always been a place for dreams, but with horses they were more so. Something happens to a man when he gets on a horse in a country where he can ride forever; it is quite easy to ascend to an impression of living in a myth. He either feels like a God or closer to God. There seems never to have been a race of plains horsemen that was not either fanatically proud or fanatically religious. The Plains Indians were both."

There is some of that left. Yes, the plains are an urban society now, judged by the fact that about one half of the people live in cities. But the land is still dominant. It sets the rhythm of life there, determines the economy, dictates the architecture and clothing, and preserves a humility and awe of God that is more apt to be lost in other regions.

A few years ago somebody figured out that the people in the plains states had roughly 200 times the living space that the citizens of metropolitan New York possessed.

A century ago one person wrote: "Like an ocean in its vast extent, in its monotony, and in its danger (the plains country) is like the ocean in its romance, in its opportunities for heroism and in the fascination it exerts on all those who come fairly within its influence." It was a land of grass so lush and strong that it scraped the bellies of the horses that the men rode. Now it is still grass but much more—corn, wheat, soybeans. There are lakes in the north and the great Missouri and Mississippi Rivers which drain its tabletops, and underground rivers that feed places like Nebraska's Sand Hills. In Texas the rivers and lakes are underground and they are oil.

Before many men had the courage to look closely at these trackless reaches, they put the western part of the plains down on maps as "The Great American Desert." It was thought to be fit only for savages. No doubt much of the thinking was influenced by the weather. Violent and extreme, it rushes in on the unwary, who feel naked before its onslaught.

Tracks of the Sante Fe Railroad recede into the Kansas distance. They brought adventurers and settlers to the raw land and also great wealth for the men who built them.

Hail can batter a wheat crop in the middle of a scorching summer day. Those who lived through them cannot forget the dust storms that blew in from the west, sifting the fine grit through windows and doors, into every crevice, blotting out the sun and then leaving an ochre sky to taunt the ground dwellers.

Ice storms still fell thousands of telephone poles, and every winter even in these times blizzards strike the prairies with a ferocity that stuns the senses of those caught in them. One resident of a modern town on the plains felt himself being "smothered" by the huge snow flakes driven against his face. The snow was so clotted by the howling wind he could not see his hand inches from his face. He had no sense of direction and groped in the white void foot by foot through his own yard until like a blind stranger he found the door to his home. He learned later that a farm wife not many miles away had frozen to death in the same storm, "lost" 50 yards from her house.

When there is not snow there may be rain, unmerciful, pounding rain, in buckets and barrels. Sometimes it cannot run off and it brings devastation as in Rapid City, South Dakota, in 1972 when more than 200 people died from a deluge. The wind itself is menacing. Tornadoes lash the horizon in the spring and summer, their death-dealing funnels rising and falling, splintering trees and buildings that lie in their paths, driving straws through timbers as if to show those who dare live on the plains how insignificant they can be before nature's fury. Even in tranquil times the wind blows, restlessly caressing the grass, the tiny towns. There is a story that a new visitor years ago asked a plainsman if the wind was always so severe. "No, mister," his host replied, "it'll blow this way for a week or ten days, then it'll take a change and blow like hell for a while."

But as always in the legend, the worst is exaggerated, the normal passed by. There is beauty and calm in the plains. Mark Twain found fulfillment on his river. Thomas Hart Benton, the painter, has captured the sense of bounty that the plains yield up. Grant Wood saw and painted the forms and people of the plains, etched by a sun that is unhindered as it sweeps across the land, bringing life. "When spring comes again," a pioneer wrote, "when soft green covers the vast expanses . . . when bounteous crops . . . luxuriantly spring forth . . . when the wild prairie grasses provide sustenance for the grazing herds; then everything else is forgotten."

Well, not quite everything else. Loneliness was perhaps the greatest enemy. People could protect themselves from most of the extremes of weather, and they did. But hearts died in the long days of the early pioneers when they heard and saw no other humans. O. E. Rolvaag, writing of the northern plains in *Giants in the Earth* caught the feeling. Per Hansa's wife, Beret, cringed from the vastness around her. "Could no living thing exist out here, in the empty, desolate, endless wastes of green and blue? she asked herself. How could existence go on, she thought desperately? If life is to thrive and endure, it must have something to hide behind." From the Dakotas to Texas is 1,500 miles and a lot of differences along the way but historian Walter Prescott Webb found the same thing. "Men loved the plains . . . There was zest to the life, adventure in the air," he wrote. "But what of the women? There was too much of the unknown, too few of the things they loved . . . The loneliness which women endured on the Great Plains must have been such as to crush the soul . . ."

No more. The plains states became the region of hometowns. They were the shopping centers for farms in some cases. But in many instances towns were laid out and started by railroads and real estate speculators whose vistas of teeming cities and great wealth were unending. Those without a solid economic base struggled and died, or limped along due to their birth defects. Many never got off the blueprints. The land speculators were often unscrupulous. Vertical river banks were sold for building lots to New Yorkers. Sites a hundred miles from a major waterway were advertised as river ports.

Many of the towns did grow and furnished their residents with a life that has been the subject of study by sociologists and the grist for authors. Mark Twain glanced back at his boyhood in Hannibal, Missouri, and summed it up as "full of liberty, equality and Fourth of July." Television commentator Eric Sevareid, who grew up in Velva, North Dakota, also had good words for his days in the hometown. "No man had the power to direct another to vote this way or that . . . This was an agrarian democracy, which meant that there was no concentration of capital goods, which meant in turn, since we had no all-powerful landlords, that no class society based upon birth or privilege had a chance to develop."

Every time that William Allen White, of Emporia, Kansas, sat down at his typewriter he renewed his love affair with Kansas. He marveled at the spring wild flowers, sniffed the summer breezes with relish. So deft was his touch at the typewriter, that he became a national voice in the Republican party, a friend and counselor to Presidents. He went back to Emporia after every journey, relieved to be home. The small communities of the plains, he wrote, "house their citizens more satisfactorily, give them more breathing space, provide more of the physical and spiritual blessings of life . . . for the average citizen than any other kind of human habitation."

Sinclair Lewis, who grew up in Sauk Centre, Minnesota, saw things differently. His *Main Street* was a savage satire on his hometown. Gopher Prairie, the name of the town in Sinclair's work, was a repository for scorn, ridicule, and anger against what he saw as a materialistic and intellectually sterile existence. His town was one dimension, selfish and graceless. His heroine, Carol Kennicott, saw the town's ideal as "cheap labor in the kitchen and the rapid increase in the price of land. It plays cards on a greasy oil cloth in a shanty, and does not know that prophets are walking and talking on the terrace."

How could intelligent men like White and Lewis get so far apart? The answer lies somewhere deep within each one and the inexorable forces of the plains that shape men.

As the farm population fell dramatically after World War II, many of the towns simply went dead. There was no business. Others, however, hung on and like McCook, Nebraska, and Northfield, Minnesota, brought in new industry. Having a broader economic base meant new life for these towns. Now, superhighways link them to larger cities. Television brings the faraway world to their quiet streets. The appeal of small town life is once again growing.

Fred Maroon roamed the plains' vastness from the Dakotas to Texas, 1,500 miles deep and 750 miles wide. His first picture was of corn, the

A church supper in Central City, Nebraska. This is one of those quiet rites of rural society that binds people together and to their land.

golden bounty of Iowa. Nearly a billion bushels a year come from the Iowa farms. Most of the corn is fed to livestock and Iowa pork and beef are something special in the national diet. Indeed, though Iowa is lumped in with the plains states it has always seemed different. Richard Rhodes wrote that Iowa was "more a demonstration farm than a place; more some cosmic public relations project designed to prove that God's in his heaven and all's right with the world . . . Iowa might have been buttered, it is so sleek." Poet Robert Frost, who lived on New England's rocky slopes, once looked at Iowa's thick, black soil and said: "It looks good enough to eat without putting it through vegetables."

The western parts of Iowa begin to shade into more typical plains. And by Nebraska and Kansas there is the famous horizon. Here is the sound of distant train whistles, the thin mark of rails receding into the western sun. Maroon took his picture in Kansas City. The late afternoon sun glints off the tracks etching in gold the web of steel where the long trains of the plains are made up, dismantled and shuffled in the cycle of supply. The Santa Fe was one of those rail lines which was born in the prairie out of equal parts of vision and greed. In its early years it spawned Dodge City, Kansas, where Wyatt Earp walked and legend was made. Dodge City was so instantly sinful and riotous that, for lack of a conventional jail, a huge hole was dug 15 feet in the ground and the offenders lowered into it to cool off.

The Santa Fe System began as the Atchison & Topeka, the dream of a Pennsylvanian named Cyrus Kurtz Holliday who went to Kansas in 1854. There was no limit to hopes in those years, in that space. Holliday staked out Topeka, had it proclaimed the territorial capital, then he thought it might be a good idea to have a railroad start in his town and run down the old cattle trail to Santa Fe. It was built in spurts with the usual number of battles, legal and armed, but eventually ran from the Great Lakes to the Pacific, part of the stitching of the nation, a vision come true. Among other things that it produced was Fred Harvey, whose hotels, restaurants and dining cars became a part of western legend.

The Santa Fe was not the first or the greatest or the most difficult of American rail systems. But it played its part in bringing settlers to the plains, in building cities and binding west and east in an irrevocable union. There are no other stories in American development that rival the building of the railroads for audacity, daring and outrage. There are no other developments that hurried America toward her fulfillment as much as the railroads.

The St. Louis Gateway Arch commemorates the conquering of the western wilderness by men and their machines. The 630-foot structure, sheathed in stainless steel, is the design of Eero Saarinen, a tribute to St. Louis' modern renaissance. In the 1950's the old river city was down at the heels. An English author called it a "dump." Then the people stood up, shook themselves, and changed things. They wiped out slums whole blocks at a time, built new homes and office buildings, added a sports arena, parks and to top it off built the arch on the old Mississippi River levee. St. Louis is a legend of change. It began as a fur-trading center, then was the way station for explorers and settlers going west. When steamboating's golden age began on the Mississippi, St. Louis had a population of 4,977. By 1870 it was the third largest city in America and its levee was crowded with steamboats. Then came the railroads. It didn't matter to St. Louis. The first bridge across the river to Illinois in 1874 simply meant another opportunity. By the turn of the century St. Louis was making beer, shoes, stoves, clothing and wagons. In 1904, she put on one of the grandest spectacles of the time, the Louisiana Purchase Exposition. The world had never seen such a fair. At a cost of $40 million there were lagoons, formal gardens and exhibits that included the electric stove, wireless telegraph and the dial telephone. Some say the ice cream cone and the hot dog were invented in the Exposition's amusement area.

In that progressive atmosphere it was easy to forget that St. Louis' trade had once been principally with the Indians, whose tragic history makes them seem like abused actors in the American saga. Without them in their war paint riding their tough ponies against the cutting edge of civilization the western stories would have been pale accounts of boring marches and wagon trains. After playing their parts, the Indians were dispossessed and forced into desolation of land and spirit. Maroon's Indian portrait is of a descendent of the Cherokee Tribe, now in Oklahoma.

P 169   Cattle auction, Central City, Nebraska.

Pp 170-171   Country church, Ralph, South Dakota.

Pp 172-173   Badlands National Monument, South Dakota.

Pp 174-175   Theodore Roosevelt National Memorial Park, North Dakota.

Pp 176-177   The Apache Belles in the Cotton Bowl, Dallas, Texas.

The story of the Cherokees is one of those episodes in the grim chronicle. President Andrew Jackson in 1829, with the approval of Congress, decided that all of the southern Indians should be moved west of the Mississippi. Jackson felt that the Indians could never be absorbed into white man's society, even though the southern tribes had shown remarkable adaptability. Some lived in log cabins, wearing homespun clothes, farming like their white neighbors, with whom there was some intermarriage. It was not good enough for Jackson and his supporters. By decree of the United States government, some 60,000 original Americans with more right to the land they occupied than anyone, were deprived of their forested homelands, sent under armed guard to a treeless plain in the western unknown. Later it would be called Oklahoma. The move for the Cherokees, the most advanced and peaceful of the Indians, came in 1838. They were rounded up at gunpoint, taken off their farms in Tennessee and Georgia, placed in camps and then marched west by the military. Their ranks were decimated by strain and disease. One out of four of the Indians died on the march. The 14,000 who survived the Trail of Tears rallied remarkably, began to rebuild their society with a three-part government, schools and a newspaper. It was not many years before the whites began to covet the new lands of the Cherokees and the promise of Jackson that this land would be "guaranteed to the Indian tribes as long as they shall occupy it" was strained and broken.

The flood of white men inundated everything, even the land ocean that seemingly could hold the world. All of those empty miles now are carefully fenced and cropped, and towered over by grain elevators. The elevators are the banks for the great wealth of the plains. Maroon found that the one he photographed in Kansas seemed to rise out of the distance just as the cathedral at Chartres grows from its village. All concrete and efficiency, the elevators can swallow up millions of bushels of harvested wheat, dry it, then disgorge it into waiting trains on the sidings, which will take it to millers in the cities. The vertical lines of the elevators are sometimes the only challenge to the horizontal panorama of the plains. Beneath the shadows of these elevators the people

185

The first white man to see the Missouri was shaken. Father Jacques Marquette, canoeing down the Mississippi in 1673, came to the point where the Missouri empties into the Mississippi. It was an angry, turbulent scene that prompted the Father to write he had seen "nothing more frightful, a mass of large trees entire with branches, real floating islands . . . so impetuous that we could not without great danger expose ourselves to pass across. The agitation was so great that the water was all muddy, and could not get clear."

Nearly three centuries later the people along the Missouri were still fearful of the river when spring came. In 1952 General Lewis A. Pick, co-author of the plan to control the Missouri, landed in Omaha to help battle the spring flood which was building up from melting snow far to the north. When the predicted deluge swept down the valley, spreading as wide as seven miles in some points, General Pick pronounced it "the greatest flood that white man has seen come down the Missouri Valley." They worked feverishly in the cities to build up the dikes and in most instances, aided by the Engineers' expert predictions of the flood crests, contained the river. Yet, some two million acres of farm land were flooded, 130,000 residents driven from their homes. This was impetus to finish off the Pick-Sloan plan's six huge dams that brought the Missouri under control, the river's spring outpouring then being stored in vast reservoirs and released slowly to generate power and irrigate crop land. This kind of reshuffling of geography typifies the vision and ambition that the men and women of plains have always possessed.

Not all the land of the plains can yield lush crops and fat animals. Plenty is not the universal symbol. Nowhere is barrenness so blatant in the plains as in the Badlands of South Dakota. And yet even here there is a parched beauty which has produced a crop of tourists. Forty million years ago it used to be an area of marshes and sluggish rivers. Layers of clay, sand and mud were washed down from the higher Black Hills. These deposits were gashed by erosion and when the climate turned semi-arid the peaks and ravines became spectacles of banded color that changed as the sun moved overhead. Maroon found them more vivid than ever when wet from a rain storm.

His picture of Theodore Roosevelt National Memorial Park is at daybreak, the fog filling the valleys of the rugged North Dakota hills, clouds lingering above. It was the kind of scene that Roosevelt relished. He went to the Little Missouri River for his health and found not only the kind of air and men he liked but an exuberant philosophy that would help make America a great power after he became President. Roosevelt established his ranch in 1883 with the idea that it was to be a paying concern. He like many others suffered from the illusions of the open range, which among other ideas fostered the notion that cattle would more or less multiply effortlessly in country where there was water and grass. The winter of 1886-87 burst that bubble. It was the worst that white man had ever recorded in the northwest and it wiped out half of Roosevelt's cattle. Yet even after such commercial disappointment, he kept coming back to ride and camp. He sold out in 1898 just before going to Cuba with his Rough Riders but he carried the memories of his joyous cowboy days with him for life.

In these times the cowboys who turn people on out west are more apt to play football than ride horses. In Dallas the Cowboys are expected to be consistently among the best teams in the National Football League. Texans would have it no other way. At New Years much of Texas seems to focus on the Cotton Bowl and the game of football which Maroon photographed. The sports palaces are spectacles of opulence. Some of the special suites in Dallas' new arena were sold to the wealthy for $50,000 and more than that was spent to decorate them to the taste of their owners. The Apache Belles are a kind of Texas extravagance, too. They are smiling, well endowed young ladies who display their special graces at the half times. And on the field is the kind of contest of brute strength and brains that Texans still like to believe they represent.

Just as these people, rich from oil, cotton and cattle, are buying sports excellence, they are also creating culture out of their wealth. They have poured millions into museums and art centers. In Houston, which calls itself the world's space capital, the lobby of the Jesse Jones Hall for the Performing Arts extends the theme. From the ceiling hangs a gleaming

sculpture by Richard Lippold called "Gemini II," which is a tribute to man's reach for the moon.

Perhaps the story of Texas is best illustrated in Maroon's picture of polo in Midland. In the background are the refinery towers, the profile of the vast wealth of Midland. In the foreground, the men of Midland thunder over the turf of their polo field in a contest of horses and riders that is still considered more European than American. Polo had been played elsewhere in Texas, but when it arrived in Midland, it arrived with gusto. A multi-millionaire enthusiast named George Landreth headed a drive in 1965 to construct five polo fields. In two years they were completed. The next year Landreth's team won the United States National Open Championship. The secret, according to one Midland polo enthusiast, is plenty of good weather, plenty of space, plenty of money. That is the modern profile of Texas.

"San Antonio," wrote Larry McMurtry, "is of Texas, and yet it transcends Texas in some way, as San Francisco transcends California, as New Orleans transcends Louisiana. Houston and Dallas express Texas—San Antonio speaks for itself . . ."

It is old—founded in 1718. It is quiet in a way that few other Texas cities are quiet. It has its own character given by the Spanish who settled it, preserved and flavored by the Germans who came later. It was the capital of the old province of Texas before it was a part of the United States. The Alamo, where the strongest legend of courage in Texas was written, is in San Antonio, faithfully preserved, its story of bravery pumped into every school boy and girl in the state. San Antonio was the first of the Texas cowtowns, the start of the famous trails like the one John Chisholm named. Teddy Roosevelt recruited some of his Rough Riders in San Antonio. And countless general officers, who became famous in the wars of this century, matured in the military bases and camps which surround San Antonio. The city does not have the flash and the gleam of Dallas and Houston. But she has something else—a character born of those dry plains before oil and the automobile. That may last the longest.

MOUNTAIN STATES

COLORADO, UTAH,
NEW MEXICO, ARIZONA, IDAHO,
NEVADA, WYOMING, MONTANA

The land ripples westward through the Appalachians with a certain aged dignity. It flows into the vast middle reaches and for a thousand miles quietly gathers strength. Then it rises inexorably to its climax—the Rocky Mountains.

Their mystery and promise pulled a population from the comfortable valleys and meadows of the east. Their freedom and challenge developed one of the most romantic and fearless fraternities of Americans ever— the mountain men. And still those mountains lure millions of modern tourists who come to sniff a bit of the sparkling air, plunge down the slopes of powder snow or just look with awe at a little of God. The Rockies have defied the human hand more than any other part of this nation. Their winters are so furious that only the hardiest adventurers, intoxicated by the splendor of snow, ice and solitude, dare trespass in the remote areas in those months. For climbers caught in summer storms there can be moments of splendid terror. The thunder sounds as if it were run through a thousand stereo sets as it ricochets along the ridges. Trees shatter and crash when the lightning rages and sometimes eerie balls of fire roll off the crags and one's hair stands on end.

Mark Twain, who was so wise and sentimental about this nation, drank in the sight from the Rockies and wrote, "We were in such an airy elevation above the creeping populations of the earth that . . . it seemed that we could look around and abroad and contemplate the whole great globe."

A favorite Colorado story is about Texas Governor Allan Shivers' boast that Texas was twice as big as Colorado. Dan Thornton, then Colorado's Governor, replied: "Take another look, partner. When you lay our

P 191   Shooting the rapids on the South Platte River, near Denver, Colorado.

Pp 192-193   The San Juan Mountains in the Rockies, near Ouray.

Pp 194-195   Bryce Canyon National Park, Utah.

Pp 196-197   Sundown and stillness Taos mission church, New Mexico.

Pp 198-199   Where the air is clear the view unhindered. White Sands National Park, New Mexico.

mountains out flat with all their dips, spurs and angles, you come out with a country four times as big as yours." The mountains are the continent's spine. School children still are asked to visualize how a snow flake falling on the eastern slope finds its way in the spring thaw to the Atlantic Ocean and one falling on the western slope plunges through the rills and rivers to the Pacific.

Those states which lay claim to the Rockies have deserts and farms, subtropical climate and arid reaches of alkali. But the mountains dominate. They sing the siren song of release.

John Colter was perhaps the first American who really heard it and responded. He was a member of the party of Lewis and Clark. Coming back from that famous journey in 1806, Lewis and Clark met two fur traders headed up the Missouri to trap beaver. They wanted Colter to go back into the wilderness with them as a guide and adviser. Despite the fact he had just spent two years away from civilization in the unknown west, Colter accepted. For the next four years he roamed the mountain country, the first of the mountain men. His solitary journeys were in virgin country much of the time and he was the first of his kind to see many of the spectacles of the west that now are enshrined in national parks. Colter crossed the Continental Divide at Union Pass, tramped the Snake River and saw the Grand Tetons. He came upon the hot springs and geysers near Yellowstone, escaped 500 Blackfeet Indians by outrunning them after they challenged him in a race for his life.

Today one can sense what this love affair must have been like. In the high streams water is pure enough to drink. On some days the air is so clear that those not familiar with the region are deceived by distances. The peaks that appear a 10-minute-drive away take hours to reach. Captain Zebulon Pike, for whom the peak was named, was among the first to be so confounded. In 1806 he approached the Rockies and spotted his mountain. A week later he figured he would reach it in another day. Three days later he was still walking towards it. He gave up on the crest of a foothill 12 miles away, writing in his journal, "It would have taken a whole day's march to have arrived at its base, when I believe no human being could have ascended to its pinical." According to writer Bryce

Pp 200-201 Evening light in the Grand Canyon, Arizona.

Pp 202-203 Wrangling horses in the dawn. Cowboys near Tubac, Arizona.

Pp 204-205 Silver City died with the hopes for great wealth. Some $4 million in silver was mined before the rich veins expired. Silver City is now an Idaho ghost town.

P 206 The search for easy wealth goes on in the west. Las Vegas, Nevada.

207

S. Walker that was another of Pike's many miscalculations. In 1820, Pike's Peak was climbed by three surveyors; in 1858, Julia Archibald Holmes of Lawrence, Kansas, hiked up it for a lark, wearing a calico shirt and bloomers, carrying a copy of Emerson's *Essays* and a writing kit, dragging her husband along. Taking refuge behind a boulder on the top she wrote that being there "fills the mind with infinitude, and sends the soul to God."

Today people still rhapsodize as Mrs. Holmes did about the mountain views but they also use the weather and the land in the mountain states to make their livings. There are professional hunters who roam the mountains to protect sheep and cattle from coyotes and wolves. For half a century men from the Basque country of northern Spain have been imported to central Idaho to mind the huge herds of sheep raised there. It is such a big country that some of these shepherds, who work from horses and pickup trucks, are almost entirely alone for as long as six months out of a year. The lure of the snow slopes of the Rockies to skiers is strong and growing stronger. The names of Vail and Aspen are synonymous with the best skiing in the world. Now there is even a "Mountain White House." President Gerald Ford continued his pilgrimages to Vail after he became President. The affairs of state were conducted, much to the amazement and amusement of journalists and politicians, from the deep snow of Colorado for ten days over Christmas, Ford's traditional time for vacation.

Young college men and women flock to the national parks in the summers to wait on tables or guide the tourists. There are mountain-climbing schools and full-time guides who take raft trips down the rough rivers. There is oil and lumber in that 864,000 square miles of space, much of it government owned, and vast mountain sides and prairies where citizens can wander at their will. Nevada is 86 per cent Federal land; Utah is 67 per cent; Wyoming, 47 per cent.

And these lands are dotted with other governmental footprints. Beneath the Rockies near Colorado Springs is the United States Air Force Academy, a spectacular institution established in one $200 million gesture by the government. Near Great Falls, Montana, is an Intercontinental Ballistic Missile Base, its deep silos cradling a part of the greatest destructive force that man has ever assembled. The Atomic Energy Commission has its National

The gamblers come like moths to the Las Vegas flame. On Fremont Street only the sun rising out of the desert can mute the incandescent strip.

Reactor Testing Station near Idaho Falls. Under a mountain in Colorado is the three-story combat operations center of the North American Air Defense Command.

If there is one business that symbolizes the mountain states it is ranching. It is not as important in dollars as electronics or mining but it combines nostalgic appeal with the outdoors and still is an essential industry for America's hordes of meat eaters. The Spaniards were the originators, bringing their cattle to the New World in the 1520's. The cattle evolved into the Longhorns of northern Mexico and Texas. After the Colorado gold rush of 1859, they showed up in the Rockies. Now the cattle fatten on millions of acres of private and public lands where grazing is allowed. They are tended from jeeps and helicopters and the cattle barons who used to deal with handshakes and a grunt or two use computers and complex contracts. But the business goes on mostly in the out of doors and it still kindles imagination. The ranchers who long ago gave up the Longhorns for such sophisticated meat producers as the blocky, white-faced Herefords, remain a colorful, outspoken breed of men who brag about their push-button feeding operations like they do their mountain air. There are now upwards of 20 million cattle on the ranches of the mountain states.

Not quite so colorful, but perhaps more important to modern society is the mining industry. It produces more than a billion dollars a year of essential ores—uranium, copper, lead, zinc, silver, vanadium, mercury, molybdenum, gold. Arizona accounts for almost half of the copper dug in the United States. Nearly half of the country's silver comes from Idaho. The Climax Mine in Colorado yields by itself half of the molybdenum produced in the nation. Molybdenum is used to make high-strength steel. Gold, of course, was the original discovery which brought the miners hurrying west. It was discovered in 1859 in Colorado and Nevada and three years later in Montana. For the rest of that century almost everybody in the region was preoccupied with the search for gold and silver. Copper ore at one time was considered a relatively worthless commodity which got in the way of gold and silver mining. Then came the telephone and Thomas Edison's light bulb. Copper wire was found to be the best thing for carrying power and voice impulses. The industrialists began to lace the world with copper wire. In the continuing search for copper the miners dug the world's largest man-made excavation. It is in Bingham, Utah, a terraced hole that measures two miles from rim to rim and half a mile deep. It has produced more copper—nearly 10 million tons—than any mine in the world's history. It has given up so much gold just as a by-product that it is the nation's second largest gold mine. The demand for lead was spurred by America's love affair with indoor plumbing. Zinc was needed for storage batteries. As steel production became more sophisticated the maws of industry demanded more molybdenum. Then came the nuclear age and the need for uranium.

For all of their lusty value, minerals are not nearly so important to the mountain states as water. Life simply could not go on without the immense system of water control and use which has been devised for the dry segments of the mountain area. The Colorado River is one of the most used rivers in the world, its waters being dammed, diverted, recycled and consumed. Hoover Dam, the highest concrete dam (726 feet) in this hemisphere, is the most spectacular structure along the river, forming the 115-mile-long Lake Mead, which not only generates power and irrigates cropland but lures millions of tourists to its cool surface every year to fish, swim and boat. Man's exploitation of the Colorado is a source of conflict among those who live along it. Yet, on the stretches where nature has not been touched there is perennial beauty and interest. Rapids can be navigated in rubber rafts; the deep caverns carved out of the stone walls enthrall amateur explorers. The Colorado River is so thoroughly used by man that when it comes to the end of its epic journey in the Gulf of California it is little more than a trickle of brackish water ejected from irrigation systems.

A symphony for the spectacle of the Rocky Mountains would play on the sound of water. It ripples over the pebbles in the allegro, then spreads into quiet pools for the slow movements and crashes into the boulders for the finale. Fred Maroon began his mountain sequence with a picture of a kayak in the white water of the north fork of the South Platte River near Denver. His portrait of the mountains themselves comes

from the San Juan range of southwestern Colorado. There are a dozen peaks higher than 14,000 feet. They plunge and rise in an exciting array of formations. Author Walker climbed the San Juans and like others emerged on an intellectual and physical high. "The San Juans," he wrote, "provide more beauty than a person reasonably needs—all those convoluted shapes, those chromium colors, those humbling distances, those obliterating tonnages of earth and rock. Amid such grandiose perspectives a person's sense of scale breaks down."

Bryce Canyon, in Utah, has a special "tenderness and gentleness . . . the delicacy of it is melting," as one writer has said. Indeed, Bryce Canyon is not really a canyon at all. It is an area about three miles long and two miles wide that continues to enlarge and change from the erosion of rain and wind. Natural spires and arches appear in the sandstone, then crumble to be replaced by new ones. The colors are coral, orange and rose and they shift with the sun. Maroon's picture of Bryce is at Sunset Point.

In Taos, New Mexico, the dry, clear air is more preserver than avenger. It slides over the desert and the sun pours through it with little resistance. The environment is parched and thin and human existence has always been somewhat precarious. Yet, for those who clung to the sun there was some permanence. Their buildings at least were not smashed by storms or weathered away by rot. Maroon's subject is a mission near Taos. The architecture is Spanish, the influence, Pueblo Indian (some 1,400 Pueblos live nearby). The pristine quality of the region glows best in Maroon's picture of the moon rising above the White Sands National Monument, in New Mexico's Tularosa Basin. The purity of sand and light and air so captured Maroon that he wandered off into the dunes and for a moment lost his bearings. Others have done that, too, in the strange rapture produced by this shifting ocean of gypsum sand. The dazzling white dunes are sculpted continuously by the wind, offering a landscape that at times resembles a wilderness snowfall. The sands for all time have sifted over the tracks of men who traversed them. But they preserved arrowheads and tools and from these fragments the story of restless, sometimes tragic early life can be reconstructed. In our time the White Sands cradled this nation's first missile tests. Only a few miles away is the Trinity Site, where the world's first atomic bomb was exploded, its hideous rumble and eerie light consumed in the vast stillness of the white desert.

The silence and scale of the Grand Canyon is as much a part of this national spectacle as the rock and color that lure so many to the rim. The canyon swallows its viewers. It is a range of mountains turned upside down with space where the rock should be and rock where the space should be. The rays of a sunset bring out the subtle coloring in Maroon's picture. A mile below the rim runs the Colorado River which carved the huge sculpture. For all of the familiarity with this view, it awes almost every new beholder. There is here a taste of the forces of creation, an aura of desolation that captivates but repels at the same time.

I f there is a characteristic of this region which ranks next to the mountains themselves, it is the men. Mountain men, miners and cowboys. Of course the old trailblazers like Jim Bridger and Kit Carson are gone and so are those lonely prospectors who hit the big lodes. The cowboys, however, hang on, a fringe of men who still live in the out of doors, who still ride horses when jeeps will not do. Maroon found some of them on an Arizona ranch. It was cold and dusty and the men, lean and burned as though they had walked out of a story book. It wasn't exactly the old west with the chuck wagon and the blanket roll, only a whiff of it. These men had come from snug bunkhouses and they had downed mountainous breakfasts of eggs, ham, sausage, fried potatoes and coffee. But they did sweat and ride and occasionally herded cattle just as in the old days.

There are men still alive in the mountain states who were real cowboys, who used to sleep on the ground and drive cattle great distances before the machines came to their land. But they are old, arthritic and they huddle in their huts with linoleum floors and live with their memories. The movie legend has a seed of truth, according to writer William H. Forbis. "The American cowboy was actually a dirty, overworked laborer who fried his brains under a prairie sun, or rode endless miles in rain

P 213   Yellowstone River canyon in the park, Wyoming.

Pp 214-215   Mammoth Hot Springs, Yellowstone National Park.

Pp 216-217   Morning bliss on Yellowstone River in the park.

Pp 218-219   The Teton Mountains, Grand Teton National Park, Wyoming.

Pp 220-221   Virginia City, Montana. Restored frontier mining town where once 200 people were murdered in six months.

Pp 222-223   Upper St. Mary's Lake, Glacier National Park, Montana.

P 224   Winter snow, Monument Valley, Arizona.

and wind to mend fences or look for lost calves," he wrote. "The high time of the American cowboy lasted a bare generation from the end of the Civil War until the mid-1880's when bad weather, poor range management and disastrous cattle-market prices forced an end to the old freewheeling ways." Forbis calculated there were only about 40,000 of them. And yet, he insists, the facts and the statistics should not be allowed to dim their stage presence in their era. Forbis goes to the diary of George Duffield, who drove a herd of Longhorns to Iowa in 1866, to show why young boys still dream of the cowboy's heroics: "Upset our wagon in River & lost many of our cooking utencils . . . was on my Horse the whole night & it raining hard . . . Horses all give out & Men refused to do anything . . . Awful night . . . not having had a bit to eat for 60 hours . . . Indians very troublesome . . . Hands all growling and swearing—everything wet and cold . . . "

Almost anything living had to struggle in those days, in that land. The American bison almost did not make it. The animal deserves some attention for its noble struggle. At first, it ruled the plains and much of the mountain area. Estimates have been made that there were 90 million buffalo (the Americanized name for bison). Those who saw them then said that they came in rivers and seas and oceans. Animals stretched from horizon to horizon sometimes, and when they ran the earth shook. Some authorities insist that no other continent has ever produced a wild game animal in such great numbers. For that very reason they were squandered. They were shot for sport, food and for no reason other than just to kill. By the beginning of this century those millions had been reduced to a mere 300. In one hunt in 1850 there were a thousand men, women and children. A good hunter could fell 250 beasts in a day. William F. Cody won his sobriquet "Buffalo Bill" by killing 4,280 animals in one 17-month period. They were shot from horseback, on foot, even from the windows of trains. Now, buffalo are being nurtured in parks and game preserves and there are more than 20,000 in the United States and Canada, shaggy, stoic reminders of the past.

The people most often defeated by the mountain states were those who wanted to dig up the wealth and cart it off to other places. The majesty

The National Bison Range, Ronan, Montana. Some 90 million American buffalo once roamed North America. About 20,000 remain, carefully tended and protected in places like Ronan.

of scenery around them was not enough. They wanted to be rich beyond any dreams that they had ever had. A few were lucky and got there. Most scraped their pathetic trenches along the rocky slopes and then left. The ghost towns are the tombstones of these extinguished hopes; Maroon found Silver City, Idaho, to epitomize them. Begun in 1860, Silver City grew to 4,000 as the rich silver veins were exploited, almost $4 million being taken from the mountain sides before they gave out. There were general stores, hotels, meat markets, a jeweler, lawyers, doctors, a newspaper, tailor shop, lumber yards, bottling plant and at least eight saloons. The sporting area of the town was called "Virgin's Alley" and the luxury of some of the "ladies" houses surpassed that of the residences of Silver City. The decline and fall of such towns was a human tragedy. Lives were pinched. Vision vanished. Silver City lost its position as county seat in 1935. In 1942, it expired totally. Its buildings stand, forming a remarkably intact shell that tells a story of a life that used to be. Maroon stood in its silence and traced its profile from the weathered buildings. There was a school and church as well as the saloons, the classic contrast in American habitation. Tucked into its mountainside it must have had a rapid pulse in its prime. The sound of horses and men, of children and dogs had to echo through its short streets. But the mountains won. They snuffed out the sustenance. The people passed on.

They stopped in such places as Las Vegas. There the climate is more salubrious, some of the laws still as relaxed. The gold and silver can be mined from the pockets of the people at the gaming tables—almost a billion dollars a year for the state of Nevada alone. The people who crowd the casinos are a different breed from the mountain men who first saw that distant land. They perhaps have some of the same cunning, the same zest for adventure of a kind. Space and air and vistas to soothe the eye are not on their minds, however. They leave the sun outside, lurk beside the roulette wheels and dice tables so long that night and day blend and there is no beginning and no end to time. Maroon came upon Las Vegas after being in the mountains and it was a profound shock. The clothes were riotous and yet the people who wore them seemed manufactured and encased in plastic, the result of a monstrous mechanical hoax. There was little joy in the casinos, a kind of nervous ritual of winning and mostly losing that only created a desire to do more of the same. Maroon fled for the sunlight.

He found it in Cheyenne and the Frontier Days, perhaps the grandest and gaudiest of the home town celebrations that this country has to offer. There he gloried in the reassurances he needed. Old and young, black, red and white mixed in a spectacle of smiles, bands and American flags. They ate and sang and rode the broncos, paraded their bikes and automobiles and relived their pioneer heritage in the easy present. "It was marvelous just to be a part of it," recalls Maroon, "it belied the problems that are blared forth in the headlines every day in the megacities."

If there is an enduring single image of mountains and rivers, tumbling falls and natural spectacles of all kinds, it is Yellowstone National Park. It is the world's first such park, established in 1872, and remains an unsurpassed display of canyons, geysers, mud volcanoes and wildlife. It is no longer really wild. There are 500 miles of public roads and there are traffic jams on the roads. There are hotels and gift shops and the places to fish for trout are marked as well as the restrooms. But the natural beauty survives in the fashion of a laboratory.

The Yellowstone River Lower Falls is the postcard scene that may be as famous as Old Faithful. Maroon took his picture at the falls, looking down the canyon. For all the people in their air-conditioned sedans who rim the edges, the river keeps on performing with dignity and beauty. It pours over the moody falls, the canyon walls sending back the roar of water and sometimes the echo of thunder from the protesting clouds that form overhead and glower, then smash against the mountains, breaking up so the sun can reclaim the rock walls, stained yellow by iron deposits that gave the park its name.

If Yellowstone is relatively tame in the summer with only an occasional bear clouting a curious tourist, it retains its full manhood in the winter. The remote areas of the park are closed when the snows come along with the wind that chills to 60° below. To some of the few who get to see it, the beauty is even greater in the snow. In 1973 two young men decided that they wanted to see and feel the wilderness such as John Colter had when he wandered there in the winter months of 1807. For 17 days they snowshoed through December blizzards, hiked over iced mountains and gazed on unruffled herds of elk in the snow-choked valleys. Beau Westover and Mark Stearns traveled 175 miles in Yellowstone and Grand Teton National Parks, suffering from the frigid assaults of the storms. But their exhilaration transcended the aching cold and fatigue. They saw "a crippled moose, its head cocked, belching steam . . . A half dozen coyotes follow(ed)." From one pinnacle their naked eyes swept horizons 200 miles distant. "More of the earth than I have ever seen from one spot," wrote Westover. Elk loom up "like goblins on the moor . . . thousands of animals weaving through the falling snow . . . as far as we can see."

In the deepest freeze of winter Yellowstone's hot springs do not subside. Maroon pictured them bubbling away as they have for centuries, forming and reforming the terraces of calcium carbonate that come from the dissolved limestone in the hot water. "It was a bit of hell turned inside out," suggested Maroon when he saw and smelled the Minerva Terrace.

Once out of its canyon the Yellowstone River grows more serene and it finally flows unprotesting into Yellowstone Lake. It is a big lake in a big (3,400 square mile) park and even in summer when tourists swarm like locusts there are places and moments for solitude. Maroon found a lone fisherman on the river at daybreak. Ahead of the horde, this man sensed his privilege, casting leisurely in the gathering light, savoring the seminal ritual of first sun in the mountains.

Just below Yellowstone is Grand Teton National Park, whose mountain profile probably makes the most indelible impression on those who see it of any range in the United States. They are mountains without foothills, as the picture shows. They jut spectacularly out of meadows and lakes. Just as tourists come and marvel today, the Indians and the early mountain men made their way to the Tetons to rest and take pleasure.

On up north is Virginia City, Montana, another of those human artifacts left to commemorate the riotous days of gold prospecting. Virginia City is perhaps one of the best restorations in the west, showing just how a frontier mining town looked and worked. The legend of Virginia City

contains a dash of candor about our early history that some other places like to bury. Many of the men who streamed into the mountains in 1863 were brutal soldiers of fortune driven by greed. In one half-year period history has it that nearly 200 people were murdered. The more law-abiding miners took things into their hands, formed a group of vigilantes and hanged 21 of the criminals and their leader, the sheriff. Not even that wave of righteousness could save the city from demise. When the gold gave out, so did the incentive to live there. Now 149 residents keep Virginia City open for tourists. But the authenticity of the restorations can conjure up some of the old flavor when some prospectors, so they say, could shake gold nuggets out of the roots of the sage brush that grew on the mountain sides.

There were no such goings on in Glacier National Park at the top of Montana. Too barren and too cold. Even today many of those who go to see the stark beauty of the park hurry away to more comfortable surroundings. Maroon paused for his picture at St. Mary's Lake. The air seemed especially clear, scrubbed of fog and mist by the latitude. The sun had little to give it pause. The shadows were clean cut and deep, the light patches brilliant. There was the message there of raw weather, a warning of hardship. He found in these youthful mountains the tracks of creation—sharp juts of rock, ragged ledges still not smoothed by wind and water. The living glaciers of the park are small but some of them easily accessible, though all of the glaciers (like others of western America) are steadily diminishing in a warming process that has many scientists concerned. Warming is not discernible to visitors, however, who can, even in summer, feel the bite of the wind on the high mountain roads.

A thousand miles away there was no wind bite to hinder Maroon's quest for pictures. In Monument Valley Navajo Tribal Park, in Arizona and Utah, red sandstone towers rise as high as 1,000 feet off the valley floor, sign posts of a timeless, relentless erosion. Nothing was more impressive to Maroon than the quiet. The small stirrings of nature suddenly became a chorus. A gentle breeze could speak. There was a fragrance and a soft caress, almost sensual for the solitary photographer. "I understood," he says, "how religions began."

PACIFIC STATES

CALIFORNIA,
OREGON, WASHINGTON,
ALASKA, HAWAII

What was named for peace is in constant contention. What was supposed to pacify, spawned greed. The magnificent works of nature are still being dismantled and replaced by the dubious projects of men. Battles rage over river water and the natural settings of mountain valleys. The beaches in some places are still breathtaking in their sweep and purity but elsewhere cut and bled, barnacled with habitats. The sun, which was the universal solvent for age and pain, the heavenly counterpart of the youth and opportunity below, has been obscured by the noxious fumes of the people who came and clustered in search of its blessed light and warmth.

Yet, for all of that there is so much that remains to glory in the Pacific states, including Alaska and Hawaii, that it boggles the mind. The voice of John Muir, one of America's greatest conservationists, is heard louder than ever along the shores and in the mountains of California, which for all of its anguish is the flagbearer of our Pacific kingdom. Muir's spirit has stayed the destruction of towering redwoods. It has halted the plans for ranks of condominiums on the bluffs of the southern beaches. The Sierra Club, which he helped found in 1892, is a national power in the preservation of wilderness and in the battle against dissipation of all our natural areas. "Climb the mountains and get their good tidings," said the bearded Muir. "The winds will blow their own freshness into you, and the storms their energy, while cares will drop off like autumn leaves." It was Muir who rhapsodized the beauties of Yosemite Valley and persuaded the Congress to make it a national park in 1890. The park struggles now against the inroads of a mobile and disposable culture. But above the traffic jams and the trailer camps, beyond the roars of the motorcycles is a

P 231   Sentinel of the Pacific. The Golden Gate Bridge in the evening. San Francisco, California

Pp 232-233   San Francisco Bay from Ghirardelli Square, a modern shopping complex made from a chocolate factory site.

Pp 234-235   Mark Taper Forum of the Los Angeles Music Center, glittering symbol of the city's best-known industry— entertainment.

Pp 236-237   Mission Bay. San Diego, California.

Pp 238-239   Western wildness. The Oregon coast, now preserved and protected.

concentrated area of natural spectacle that is unmatched anywhere in the world.

The bounty of California is so lush that since 1943, it has been the nation's number one farming state. More than 200 crops are grown in California. Though it is known more for its citrus production, the top crop is cotton, made possible by irrigation, part of the world's most complex and gigantic system of water use and control. Dams and reservoirs, canals and aqueducts are the life support system for California, which was little more than mountains, grasslands and desert for 200 years of American history.

The modern history of the Pacific states began with gold. A New Jersey carpenter by the name of James Marshall was building a saw mill on the American River when he stooped, picked up a few nuggets of "goald" and took it to his employer, John Sutter, who had established the headquarters of his small empire at what is now Sacramento. Marshall and Sutter tried to smother the news but as always in the affairs of men the effort failed spectacularly. The workers at the mill site picked up more gold. Somebody wrote a letter to San Francisco. An item got in a paper. The fever mounted. One man raced through the streets of the city showing a bottle full of nuggets and yelling, "Gold, gold." That was in 1848. In the next year an estimated 80,000 men surged into the new land by boat, wagon and on foot.

The year of the "Forty-Niner" is considered one of the most remarkable in our history. The important produce, of course, was not gold but people and a region, ultimately a way of life. By the turn of the century when the fever had long been dead, the miners had taken about $2 billion of gold from California land but it was nothing compared to the riches of the merchants and farmers. In Washington and Oregon the timber industry, which had supplied lumber for the mines and homes, continued to grow; the men and women who had come from Illinois and Maryland and all the other places to strike it rich drifted north, where the huge trees needed felling for the increasing appetite of a nation building.

Those who liked warmth went south to exploit the sun. They began to grow fruit, build railroads, and pretty soon were manufacturing airplanes. They gloried in their climate and endless space and before long that was a product for the eastern and northern markets. In 1907 a group of Chicago

The Yosemite Valley was naturalist John Muir's home, both physical and spiritual. His creed, "Everyone needs beauty as well as bread," guides the conservation movement today.

moviemakers were literally rained out. They came to Los Angeles to finish a short called *The Count of Monte Cristo*. Within a decade the great and glittering era of Hollywood was in full swing. The entire rim along the Pacific has seemed like a stage since then, producing gigantic human dramas which have most often succeeded but sometimes turned to ashes. "Don't Californicate Oregon" was a slogan conceived by those—luxuriating in the relatively sparse northern reaches—to keep dispirited southerners from invading their lands. Some Californians themselves considered a total reversal of three decades of enticement and are now pressing with increasing ferocity the idea of discouraging migration to their sunny slopes. It is time.

California has been the headwaters of rebellion, yielding much that is kooky, self-indulgent and occasionally frightening. That singular culture which we call hippie for want of a better name flowered in San Francisco. It was at the start a gentle collection of alienated kids, those who had been surfeited in suburbia, drowned in automobiles, hi-fi's and motorcycles. The young people in Manhattan and Boston still feel compelled to adopt this coloration of protest. It has drifted around the world, too, like some organic cloud, dropping to earth in the tidy cities of Switzerland and the cold slopes of Nepal.

Part of California's clout, the sociologists tell us, is the loss of inhibition that comes when clothing is not required. Perhaps the pervasive symbol is that of the California surfer. Tanned, beautifully muscled, he is as free as the waves he follows. His head may be empty, but his glands are always at their peak and there is almost no sensual pleasure he has not pursued.

California's divorce rate is now three out of every four marriages. Its split families are prototypes for television programming and academic scrutiny. Young people separate themselves from family responsibility. So do the older people who seek the sun and self-gratification in retirement communities devoid of demands for community betterment. All services come with the package. What matters is what is at the club and there is plenty—dancing, painting, wine-making, riding, billiards, tennis, golf, bridge and pottery.

Topless dancers and waitresses had their origin in San Francisco. So did the bottomless girls and these innovations just like others swept west to east in short order. The motel may not have been a California invention but its use was extended and refined there. Other drive-in institutions reached their apogee in California—movies, restaurants, banks and churches. The decline of organized religion has been notable in the state. Yet, it has not been all that long ago when Aimee Semple McPherson was the hottest evangelist in the business, known from coast to coast for her remarkable powers of exhortation. She rose from the dusty confines of tent revivals to the sumptuous Angelus Temple in Los Angeles, so beloved by the thousands of followers that the whispered, even published accounts of Aimee's adulterous flings failed to shake their faith.

California also gave the nation Chief Justice Earl Warren, who presided over the Supreme Court in the 1950's and 1960's, a period which may go down in history as a time of renewal for the principles of the Constitution. And California midwifed the John Birch Society, a collection of dour political activists whose hatred for big government, the welfare state, liberals and Communists was unbounded.

From the same climate have come the physicists and astronomers of Cal Tech, Robert Hutchins and the Center for the Study of Democratic Institutions, the RAND Corporation which has helped plan our global security strategy, the Livermore Laboratory at the University of California, Berkeley, which designs nuclear weapons. Eric Hoffer is a Californian, too, a beefy longshoreman who has shunned formal education, position and wealth, but who delivers from his San Francisco park bench some of the most cogent and penetrating commentaries on our times and society.

If California has reached the change of life, then Alaska and Hawaii are carrying on her sense of adventure and opportunity. In Hawaii, east and west come together in a genial collision of climate and people. It is a haggis of mountains and beaches, volcanic desert and deluges that can soften the hardest hearts. If Alaska were laid on the old 48 states it would cover Minnesota, Iowa, Wisconsin, Illinois and the better parts of Missouri, Kansas and the Dakotas. Oil on the north slope may dwarf all its other products except one—wilderness. Alaska's untouched mountains, its unexplored glaciers are unmatched on this continent. There is no literature that embraces all of this, no thought that can carry those trackless miles from California to the far side of Hawaii, or the topmost iceberg of Alaska. There is a point of reference. It is the Golden Gate Bridge, still an invitation to adventure, and perhaps one of the most beautiful objects that man has constructed on this earth. Fred Maroon pictured it at dusk, full of majesty and its own mystery. The ships that pass under its arched span bring the flavor of the world. They sound their mournful horns as the fog swirls by to cover the bay. The Golden Gate Bridge speaks for that restless American spirit that survives, especially in the Pacific states.

The bay looks different seen from the old Ghirardelli chocolate factory, which has been turned into one of the country's most appealing shopping centers. It is Saturday afternoon in Maroon's picture and there is a good breeze across the cool water. The sail boats are racing, the people strolling along the water's edge. The good life may be San Francisco's most distinguished product. Not pictured, but behind and to the sides of the Maroon lens, is the bustle of Ghirardelli Square. It is a magnet for the immense tourist trade, its shops and restaurants jammed by those who seek a short cut to California chic. The adventurer Jack London who wrote of his wild times on the San Francisco waterfront wouldn't know the place, but he would be welcome.

The sense of the past which San Francisco has so carefully nurtured is harder to come by in California's southland. It has not been that long ago that most of the population centers were little more than towns that served the ranchers. John Gardner, the head of Common Cause, the successful grassroots political movement, was born in Beverly Hills and remembers it as a crossroads town beyond the bustle of Los Angeles, itself a formless expanse of modest bungalows. Maroon's Los Angeles picture shows the Mark Taper Forum in the Los Angeles Music Center, the symbol of the city's cultural arousal and growth. For all of that, Los Angeles' strength in the arts lies in the plethora of do-it-yourself orchestras, theatricals, rock bands and poetry groups. From these stirrings come many of the movie stars and television performers of national and world note.

Portage Glacier, Alaska. The vistas of ice and mountains in the largest state are endless, some areas less mapped than the surface of the moon.

San Diego was a naval base with superb weather which lured those who wanted a life of the least resistance. It was also a haven for aviators and scientists who needed an outdoor laboratory. When the combination of sunshine and mild, dry air became saleable, San Diego went enthusiastically into the business. Mission Bay, which Maroon photographed from the air, is one result. It is the marriage of all the southern California technical skills, gadgets, the sun and sea. It is a $100 million complex of homes, hotels, parks, beaches, restaurants, campgrounds, marinas. Its developers reclaimed beaches, carved out new channels to let in clean salt water, dredged up new islands to add interest and recreational area. Where there was once nothing much but brackish water and muck, thousands of boats take the sun worshipers through the sparkling complex of lagoons, a ritual of celebration for turning something bad into something good.

Oregonians are skeptical of such land manipulation. They have a modest amount of it but mostly they want to keep their state as natural as can be. The alarming influx of outsiders seeking to escape congestion and smog over the past years led to the singular campaign by Oregon's leaders to discourage massive new growth. The piece of the Oregon coast which Maroon found in the morning is a bit of almost 400 miles of untouched grandeur. Only 23 miles of the beach are not public property. There is a relentlessness to the Oregon coast. The wind in some areas crashes the huge breakers against rock; in other areas it rolls them smoothly up low, sandy beaches. Heavy forest comes down to the water's edge and small fishing villages cling precariously to life in that wind which seems to come from 4,500 miles of unobstructed Pacific Ocean. Maroon found the wildness impressive. "There was an exciting freshness," he said. Because of this unrestrained meeting of sea and land the cities of Oregon are inland, and the coast is left to itself and the hardy souls who savor such raw strength.

It was still more isolated in the depth of the Olympic National Park amid the patterns of moss and ferns. Maroon stayed for two hours tasting a profound aloneness. Nobody disturbed him as he worked over his camera. The sunlight did not penetrate. The northwestern rain forest is as unusual an area as any found in the United States. It is fed by as much as 150 inches of rain a year, the giant Douglas firs reaching more than 200 feet into the air, their crowns often obscured by low-hanging clouds that perpetuate the deluge. These huge trees and the redwoods and sequoias of California are the answer to the eastern skyscrapers. They humble those who walk among them. Another picture from the Olympic National Park shows its coast. It has the quality of a Japanese print and perhaps that is right because this exquisitely delicate point of the mainland reaches toward Asia.

Most of the elements of Alaska are known to us—mountains, snow and ice, water, forest. It is the size that is staggering. Man's eyes are inadequate. His normal reference points are obliterated when he tries to calculate the statistical profile of this separate world, his mind numbed when he tries to contemplate the meaning. Alaska is roughly 750 miles on a side. There are four time zones from the far tip of the Aleutian Islands to the eastern end of the Alexander Archipelago, that arm of land that reaches down along Canada. Much of the wild, cold interior has never been walked on by white man, if any man. Americans went there first for gold, then stayed for lumber, fish and escape. It became North America's outer rim of defense in World War II and the tense days of the cold war, the huge postwar military complex spawning the final surge for statehood that succeeded in 1959. And now the great hope is oil on the North Slope. There is the smell of a new boom. The crews are at work on a 798-mile pipeline that will bring the oil from Prudhoe Bay in the north to Valdez, an ice free port in the south, for shipment to the mainland. The oil will be heated to keep it from freezing and it will be pumped through the 48-inch pipe at a maximum rate of two million barrels a day. There may be 10 billion barrels of oil all told in the Prudhoe field, a reservoir of incalculable riches that was never imagined by frozen prospectors who panned for gold, then drifted into oblivion.

Alaska has a history of being used—by fortune seekers, by corporations, by the military. But she is largely unmarred. She is too big and too formidable for man to scar badly. Fort Yukon has recorded 75° below zero in the winter and 100° in the summer. The heat can melt the top layer of land into goo, while the earth below is frozen solid. The city of Anchorage can statistically support its claim to being warmer than many

On the far rim of America a lamp is lighted for evening on the beach of Mauna Kea Hotel, on the island of Hawaii.

cities in Minnesota and Wisconsin. Winter temperatures in Ketchikan are equal to those in Washington, D.C. But the snow at Valdez covers homes. At nearby Thompson Pass in the winter of 1952-53, the snowfall set a record of 975 inches, the height of an eight-story building.

Fred Maroon viewed his part of Alaska from the air, finding the jagged peaks and the great rivers of ice to form the real signature of the state. He found it a "terrible beauty," unlike anything he had seen. The peaks seemed like the fractured ends of creation, the glaciers like frozen eras.

Poet Robert Service wrote of the spell 70 years ago, of a "land where the mountains are nameless, And the rivers all run God knows where," of a "silence that bludgeons you dumb" and "snows that are older than history," of "dizzy mountains" and "deathlike valleys below . . . Some say God was tired when He made it . . . ."

Maroon flew for a full day, never seeing the same view twice, marveling at the brute beauty that turned up around each mountain flank. What he saw would hardly make a dent on a map. And some of it is probably not as well known as the surface of the moon.

If Alaska threatens and taunts, then Hawaii welcomes and comforts. The only snow and ice resides high on the mountain peaks, never able to descend the volcanic slopes where summer averages 78° and winter averages 72°. But to characterize that string of islands as an interlude of tranquility would be wrong. Their legend of love and leisure is interspersed with violence. The collision of cultures and races, which is most often held up as an example of how people should live together (there are 60 racial combinations), sometimes in the past produced tragedy. The land itself is the result of upheaval. Lava out of a gigantic crack in the floor of the Pacific built up over millions of years to form a range of subterranean mountains, of which the tops above the ocean form the chain of islands. It is abrupt land with lush green fields of pineapple, scorched cliffs, rain forests, precipices that plunge down to the blue-green sea, black beaches, arid volcanic cones and two active volcanoes.

But the reputation of languid pleasure is still dominant. Mark Twain found it and wrote in 1866 about its haunting appeal. The conventioneers

253

who now fly into Honolulu believe that they have tasted of the forbidden fruit when they disembark back home with their leis of wilted flowers draped around their necks and their bulges obscured in flowing muumuus.

Maroon's picture is of Waikiki Beach, the enduring point of contact for most mainlanders. (Twain was unimpressed, calling it "this little bathing tub of smooth water . . .") What has happened there is a source of both pleasure (for those who profit from the new hotels and concessions) and pain (for those who remember when the gracious Royal Hawaiian Hotel presided on the beach). The sun still shines, the surf still rolls bringing the foaming ridges that surfers relish. But the high-rise apartments and hotels have blunted the cooling winds, and the arcades with their shops have drowned out the soothing rustle of palm leaves. In Honolulu real estate prices have grown astronomical, sharpening the appetites of the developers for more land. There are epic struggles over the use of the waterfront among the citizens; there are traffic jams that in duration and complexity would do justice to any mainland city. But beyond the urbanized fringes there remains the land ruled by nature and the brooding presence of these slopes and valleys still casts a spell over the paved avenues and freeways.

Maroon ended his Pacific pictures not on the far tip of Hawaii, but back in California at Big Sur. A 50-mile stretch of coast below San Francisco, Big Sur has remained remarkably untouched because of its rugged character and relative inaccessibility. Many natives are fiercely dedicated to preserving this spectacular shank of the Santa Lucia Mountains. In the winter, storms spend their fury on the rocks. Fog can linger for days.

The scene is forever changing, but the ingredients are not new. They are the same as those in New England, the south, the midwest and all across the land. They are just mixed differently; parts of sun and air, rock and sea, earth and river, trees and clouds. They blend in form and color to make a country, sometimes shifting dramatically, more often subtly, from shore to forest, from plains to mountains and back to ocean. There are times, such as the one captured in this picture at Big Sur, when the sun sweeps the crevices clean, sends its warmth to the mountain sides and gentles the ocean with its golden touch.

Index of Photographs

Acknowledgments

There are many people whose assistance and cooperation were indispensable to the production of the photographs in this book. Besides the National Park Service and the curators and directors of many museums, parks, and other private and public properties represented here, I am especially grateful to the following individuals: Louis F. V. Mercier, Alice Bucher, Curtiss Anderson, Jimmy Driftwood, Cornelius W. Heine, and Bruce Williams.

F. J. M.

My text comes from the minds and the pens of countless authors and scholars as well as from my own. It is out of Fred Maroon's eye and heart. And it is a fact because of Evelyn Metzger's profound feelings about this nation. I say thanks to them all. Cassie Furgurson and Penny Marshall assembled the research for this mosaic and deserve a special tribute for competence and good cheer. I owe a special debt to the Time-LIFE books on U.S. history, the states, the wilderness and the west. They form an extraordinary repository of pertinent facts about the events, the people and places of the nation. I sampled many books by the National Geographic Society and Neal Peirce's splendid series on the states. I went to Bernard De Voto for the edited Journals of Lewis and Clark. Neil Morgan was my authority for that singular land called California. This volume, then, is like these United States—the sum of many. May it ever be.

H. S.

Jacket and typographic design by Charles O. Hyman. Book design by Charles O. Hyman adapted from an original by Allan Porter and Hans Peter Renner.

Color separations and printing by The Case-Hoyt Corporation, Rochester, N.Y.

TECHNICAL DATA

The camera most frequently used for these photographs was a Leica M4 with a 21mm Super Angulon f3.4 lens. With a few exceptions, it was supplemented by a Leicaflex SL system employing two bodies, one with a motor drive, and lenses that included the 35mm and 50mm Summicron-R, both f2; the 90mm, 135mm and 180mm Elmarit-R, all f2.8, and the 400mm Telyt, f6.8. In addition there are a few images made with the 15mm Hologon f8 lens.

All photographs were taken with existing light on Kodak film, most of which was Kodachrome. Occasionally High Speed Ektachrome film was used, and at times it was pushed beyond its standard 125 ASA or 160 ASA speed. Even at fast speeds, a tripod was used nearly always. The Kodachrome was processed by regular Kodak laboratories, and the Ektachrome by Berkey K + L, in New York City.

Custom color Dye Transfer and Ektacolor photographic prints are available of all images in These United States. *Sizes range from 11" x 14" through 40" x 60". Made from Mr. Maroon's original transparencies and signed by him, the prints are mounted on Masonite, ready for hanging. Write to Berkey K + L, 222 E 44th St., New York, N.Y. 10017.*